In Our Thirties

Insights and Expert Advice for This Decade and Beyond

LAURA SGROI
and
Thirty+ Friends

Edited by
AMY SCHLEUNES

S

S Publishers LLC
In Our Thirties: Insights and Expert Advice for This Decade and Beyond
Copyright © 2020 by Laura Sgroi
All Rights Reserved
Project Management and Editing: Amy Schleunes
Cover and Interior Design: Pamela Alegría / Sara Rodríguez-García
Author Photo: Eva Hart

Published in the United States by S Publishers LLC
ISBN 978-1-7348345-1-2
Version 1.1
Printed in the United States of America

S Publishers LLC can bring the author to your live or virtual event. For more information, to book an event, or for special discounts for bulk purchases, please contact us at +1-786-355-8780, info@laurasgroi.com or visit our website at www.laurasgroi.com.

To Claudio and Luca

Our family is the greatest gift of my thirties.

About the Author

LAURA SGROI is a certified coach and speaker who works with clients in the US, Canada, and Latin America, and has led workshops for Florida International University, Sony Music Latin, Vital Voices Miami, South Florida Fertility Expo, UP Nicaragua, Artsy Hive, and Women On Set, among other organizations. Prior to coaching, she enjoyed a sixteen+ year international career in live events, television production, and corporate communications. Her credits include Guns N' Roses, Santana, Ricky Martin, Viacom, Univision, Sony Music, Billboard, and the National Association of Television Program Executives (NAPTE). Her writing has been published in *Glamour Mexico, Glamour Latin America*, and Motherly, as well as on her website and blog. Laura holds a MA in Corporate Communications and Public Relations from Universitat de Barcelona, a BA in Marketing from Instituto Tecnológico de Santo Domingo, and a Professional Coach Certificate from the University of Miami. Originally from the Dominican Republic, she now lives in Miami, Florida with her husband Claudio and son Luca. Learn more about her at: www.laurasgroi.com.

Acknowledgments

In Our Thirties has been a collaborative idea since its inception. I want to thank with all my heart each one of the contributors who shared their stories and made me accountable to share mine. This book is yours. It exists because of you and I will be forever grateful.

During the seven years that it took to complete this book, I found some amazing human beings, including the online community built through our blog, Facebook, and Instagram pages, as well as Bennie Soto and Cindy Massey from Mindbloom, Shirley Ravachi, Regina Ravachi, Maria Gagliano, Brooke Warren, Annie Tucker, Alfredo and Elsita Ramírez, the many kind souls at Café de los Sueños, Gelateria Montebianco, Eliezer Carcache, and Los Patios Hotel, Brittany Borghi, Samantha Turner, Rob Burleigh, and Amy Schleunes, who shared her love, dedication, and commitment to writing while teaching me how to write. Margie Simo, Patricia Cedeño, Laura Barboza, Sarina Ortiz, Wendy Espinal, Daniela Guada, Eva Hart, Enrique Grullón, and Melissa Exposito used their talents to help make this book a reality. Pamela Alegría spent most of her pregnancy designing this book, making it her fourth child. Sara Rodríguez-García finished the design while in self-quarantine during the COVID-19 pandemic.

Special thanks to my Mamami, for giving me life, and every breath of yours, and for instilling in me love and respect for the written word. To my Dad, for daring me to dream, and giving me the courage to fly while making sure I stayed humble and grounded. To my sisters Amy and Carla, for being the best accomplices and for the gift of your company, support, and everything we share. To my nephews, for filling my heart with joy and pride since the day you were born. To my cousins, aunts, uncles, and grandparents, for the lovely memories. To my Italian family, for inviting me to your table, into your family, and into your hearts. To all my friends, for allowing me to be myself and loving me anyway. To Tony Parodi and the ACME family, for trusting me and changing my life and career the day you first invited me to work in the United States. To everyone who wrote a book before me, *chapeau!* To Alfonsina and Gode, my angel contributors. To Leanita, my angel consultant, for the ultimate friendship. To Granada, Nicaragua, for hosting me and giving me the time and space to write. To my husband Claudio, for your love, support, encouragement, and patience, and for believing in this book since day one. To Luca, for showing me the world through your eyes and for being the best story I have ever written, my masterpiece. Glory to God, who gave me the idea and the persistence to pursue it and make it happen. "Leave your worries to him and he will keep you firm" (Psalm 55:22).

———

"WHAT ARE THE FOUR SIGNS OF AGING?
THEY ARE WISDOM, CONFIDENCE, CHARACTER AND STRENGTH.
LOOK FOR THEM NOT WITH DISMAY BUT WITH HOPE."

Valerie Monroe, Former Beauty Director,
O, The Oprah Magazine

———

Contents

PREFACE / xiii

I. ALL THE WAY TO THIRTY / 1

II. WHAT MATTERS MOST / 15

  - PEOPLE / 17

"I wasn't seeing how I looked—I was seeing how I felt."
Autumn Whitefield-Madrano on Beauty

"Safety is not only possible, but it should be every thirty-something woman's bottom line."
Jill Di Donato on Relationships

  - HEALTH / 32

"Everyone should experiment and learn, especially people in committed relationships."
Dr. Sonjia on Sexual Health

"Fitness is a lifestyle, not just a look."
Angelique Mills on Exercise and Longevity

  - SPIRIT / 45

"Develop your ability to observe what's happening in the moment."
Warren Ogden on Spiritual Practice

  - WORK / 49

"You might have to re-evaluate your dreams."
Cindy K. Goodman on Work-Life Balance

- **MONEY / 54**

"You need to know what you want and say no to everything else."
Sandra Acosta on Personal Finance

- **LIVING / 60**

"We attract what we are or what we need to grow."
Dashama Gordon on Positivity and Sustainability

III. BACK TO BASICS / 65

IV. IN OUR THIRTIES: A COLLECTION OF STORIES FROM AROUND THE WORLD / 76

READING GROUP GUIDE / 186

Preface

On my thirtieth birthday, I set out to explore what this decade means and how best to celebrate it. I knew I was not the only one thinking about life differently at this age. I invited friends from all around the world to share their own experiences on life in our thirties. I set up a blog. I researched. I found expert contributors who could shed some light on the questions and opportunities unique to our thirties. I never imagined such an overwhelmingly positive response. Though a book was not on anybody's list, it emerged as part of this inspiring collective breakthrough.

I'm no expert, but just like you, I am living through the inspiration, insights, and issues we explore in the coming pages, and I'm happy to be your confidant as we help those of us who dreaded our thirties to see them as a time of self-discovery and growth.

I wrote this book along with thirty+ friends as an invitation to start a conversation. Please join us.

1

All The Way to Thirty

It was raining when I landed in Miami. So much for my perfectly flat-ironed hair. That morning the sun had been shining in Santo Domingo, my hometown, as we drove to the airport on the Autopista Las Américas, curving along the turquoise blue Caribbean. I was more upset than I had expected to be. I'd cried at the beauty salon, cried as I looked out at the ocean, cried in the security line as I waved to my family one last time, cried even harder on my way to the gate.

Miami was another world. The airport had ultra-modern baggage carousels with digital displays, years ahead of anything we had in the Dominican Republic. I love my country, but we're not exactly known for being on the cusp of new technology. For many years our capital's slogan was "Santo Domingo: No Problem!" But there were in fact some problems, like blackouts, unreliable public transportation, chickens and horses in the already unsafe streets, people begging for money at every other stoplight—but Dominicans don't like to dwell on problems. And why should we with all the merengue and bachata blaring from cars, entire blocks fragrant with the smells of rum and empanadas, heated conversations erupting on street corners only to stop abruptly when a confident, voluptuous woman walks by—but here in the States it was silent. The travelers, the airport workers, no one made a sound.

Four days earlier I'd turned twenty-two. I had documents to work in the US, a meager savings (I'd saved $1,000 and my dad had generously matched it), basic English, and at least one helpful contact in the entertainment industry. I was young, blindly determined, certain that nothing would stop me from succeeding—not the gray skies or my Dominican accent or the unfortunate puffiness of my hair in all that humidity. I told myself I could deal with anything.

I opened my passport and approached a US immigration agent with glossy black hair and a clean, masculine face. "Where are you traveling from?" he asked.

"Santo Domingo," I said, watching as he flipped through the pages of my passport.

"May I see your green card?" I handed it to him. Then the random questions began. "How long do you intend to stay? What's the purpose of your trip? Are you traveling alone?" I told him I was. He instructed me to turn and show him my profile, and then, in what seemed to me a clear breach of protocol, he whispered, "What I want is your number!" I thought: What? And then: Awesome! But I didn't have a telephone number yet. So he gave me his while the other passengers waited "patiently" for their turn, wondering what issues this petite alien was having with the handsome border authority.

A few days later we went on a date. My motto when it came to dating was: "If I'm not afraid of him or embarrassed by him, I'll go out with him at least once." This guy passed the test, but he wasn't a keeper, not only because I noticed his arms were shaved. Okay, that was a little weird, but he had a great body. Ten years later, after another flight from Santo Domingo to Miami, I saw him at the airport again. This time he was standing next to a Dominican woman who was holding a mixed baby. He didn't recognize me—or maybe he pretended not to. Either way, I was happy to see that he knew what he wanted and that he'd gotten it!

In Kendall, a suburb to the southwest of Miami, my new roommate Rhyna welcomed me with open arms. A psychologist, teacher, painter, and fantastic cook, she became my foster mother in Miami, and still is to this day. She'd asked my mom what my favorite meal was—*arroz con puerro* (rice with chives)—and had prepared it for my arrival. Her niece and previous roommate lent me a mattress and TV for my first week in the spare bedroom. A simple dresser stood against the far wall. Other than that the room was empty—and it was all mine. I'd grown up in a somewhat chaotic three-bedroom/two-bathroom apartment with two matriarchs—my mother and her sister—and four kids with three different last names but sharing one. Having my own room was a luxury I'd dreamed of my whole life. And my own bathroom? A gift from the gods.

I unpacked my suitcase, carefully placing my clothes in the dresser, and displayed my "Today I Sleep In" doorknob hanger, a gift from my older sister, Amy. In the mornings I'd wake up and look out my window at the men in suits rushing off to work, and the mothers taking their children to school, wondering if the rest of Miami would welcome me like Rhyna did. Did I have a place here in the States? Would it ever feel like home? Whatever happened, I promised myself two very important things: I would not forget my Spanish and I would not gain weight.

In the weeks before I moved to Miami, Amy gave me some advice: "Life only gets complicated for the things we really want to do." Honestly, I had little hesitation about complicating my life, even though I had what most Dominicans would consider a dream job. I was a production coordinator for CCF Marketing, an events agency that produced the most important shows in the country, the same shows I would stay up late to watch hours after my mom had put me to bed: awards shows, adrenaline-filled live concerts, music festivals, and presidential election specials. I got to meet the most talented artists in the Dominican Republic, including Tania Báez, a woman whose entertainment career I had admired and studied as a teenager, and to whom I once wrote a gushing fan letter (I never received a response, though I did get to tell her about it after we'd worked together for over a decade), the Dominican-York band Aventura, long before Romeo Santos became a bachata megastar, and the Mexican rock band Maná, who I'd seen as a teenager in my first-ever concert after winning tickets from a local radio station.

I had a good boss. I got four raises in two years. Suddenly I could afford meals at fancy restaurants, trendy clothing, credit on my prepaid phone, and haircuts at a professional salon. But I couldn't help thinking that production work in the US was somehow more real, more respectable. In Santo Domingo, I had to use shortcuts to avoid animals in the streets and worried constantly about being late. Traffic lights went dark during power outages. Reckless motorcyclists wove through the lanes and whipped around blind turns. At night,

I'd run to my car, afraid I'd be mugged.

American productions were different. I had worked one show in Miami in 2003, my first time in the States. The production company set me up with a room on the sixteenth floor of the old Radisson Hotel on Biscayne Boulevard. Everybody told me not to leave the hotel by myself because it wasn't a safe area, but it felt like a wonderland to me. And then I opened the curtains. My windows looked out at the MacArthur Causeway over Biscayne Bay. I saw cruise ships and private islands, luxurious homes everywhere. The bridge even lit up at night.

I was just as dazzled by the show. The crews looked relaxed and confident. They had dinner beforehand. Eating on show day? That was unheard of for me! In the Dominican Republic, I'd be running around until the last minute, photocopying, sorting, stapling, and distributing production documents. Not in Florida. And for those three days of work I was paid close to the equivalent of my monthly salary in Santo Domingo. I remember being embarrassed to cash the check at my local bank—I couldn't believe I'd been paid so much.

After that show, I began to feel trapped. Everyone else looked sort of trapped, too. I started asking the women around me: Is this your dream job? Is your husband the love of your life? Are you happy? Here's what they told me: "The love of my life was my first boy-friend. We were not allowed to date, but I will never forget him... I was once a successful model and singer, but now I can't even feed my dog, forget about my mother or daughter... At heart I am a ballet dancer, but my parents will never understand that." They all had stories of broken dreams. Though I had compassion for each of these women, they also became red flags, cautionary tales. They convinced me to move on, to not compromise, to really pursue the life of my dreams—which I knew was going to happen somewhere else.

After my first month in Miami, I had used up most of my $2,000 in savings. I was sending out hundreds of resumes and meeting with the few contacts I had from Dominican friends—a guy who worked at Telemundo, a woman who produced live events. The more people I met, the more I realized that pretty much everyone talked about the same three topics: diets, sales, and lack of time. I couldn't relate. I was at a healthy weight, I didn't have money so I didn't have to worry about shopping, and for once in my life I had all the time in the world. It was like I was living on a different planet: I was still focused on how "everything works" in the US, as my sister Amy says. Everything was so convenient. I hadn't yet realized that the hours saved due to convenience were almost always filled with more work.

A few months later, I began freelancing as a production assistant, which was techni-cally a demotion, though I never focused on that. I'd show up as casted audience for a ce-lebrity bowling show at the mall, or at a salsa dance taping, offer myself to the production team at the door, and end up working there for the rest of the week. Once, I drove a craft services van full of cockroaches through the surface streets because not even Mapquest could persuade me to take the highway. My new colleagues called me "fragile" because there was one task I was not willing to do: lift heavy objects. But I'd do anything else—working the "ticket office" behind the gates for concerts in low-income neighborhoods, "Radio Girl" signing in and out five hundred walkie talkies for a live show, catering coordinator, talent coordinator, office manager. In between gigs, I bought candles at Publix and lit them for the work gods and saints while reading the prayers printed on the label.

Despite my financial situation and the fact that my first Capital One credit card had a two hundred dollar limit, I compiled a detailed list of everything I wanted: a steady job, the ability to travel, to become an American citizen, a master's degree, and a car, laptop, TV, DVD player, radio, Palm Pilot (remember those?), and cellphone with email (what a novelty!). I told myself I would have it all by twenty-five, and if I wasn't engaged by then, I would buy myself my own diamond. And a new car. And I would own an apartment in Miami, Los Angeles, or New York, though I'd never visited the latter two.

Then came a big break: the 2004 MTV Video Music Awards Latin America. Then the Fox Sports Awards, then Premio Lo Nuestro, then the Selena tribute show. Little by little, I crawled my way back to the title I'd had when I left the Dominican Republic. Once again I was in charge of doing the impossible, making producers' and everyone's dreams come true, pulling off champagne events with Coca-Cola budgets, serving as the on-set psychologist and resident choreographer, battling only the constraints of time on days and nights that always seemed way too short.

One day my Peruvian colleague at MTV asked me about Italian guys while we were watching the World Cup matches at the office (we did do actual work, too—I promise). I told her I'd tried to date an Italian a few years back, a teacher from Sicily at the Italian school where I worked as a teenager. I first saw him at a school play. He was the tall, skinny guy with the serious face who knew how to merengue. We danced to one song, and I learned that his name was Claudio. The next morning, I showed up to assist a class. I didn't know who was teaching. Then Claudio walked in. He was wearing sunglasses and seemed like he'd had more fun than he should have the night before.

Turns out that was the case most Saturday mornings—but he was a good teacher, and he was tall. Did I mention that?

Claudio and I lived close to each other, and he started offering me rides in his blue vintage two-door Jeep. One day he invited me to lunch. We shared penne and gnocchi, tiramisu and gelato, limoncello and espresso. Domenico Modugno played in the background. I could have sworn that he wanted to kiss me—but no, it didn't happen. Six months of shameless flirting later, I decided to move on.

"Google him," my coworker said. I typed his name, expecting to find him in Australia, surfing by day and bartending by night. There he was. "Let me see, let me see," she said, rushing from her desk to my computer. I showed her the pale, skinny guy, my index finger shaking. "He looks good," she told me, clearly not that impressed.

But I was. I wrote to the organizer of an event where Claudio had worked, asking him to put us in touch. Claudio wrote back a short, professional message. He didn't remember my name, but he figured he should reply because I was writing from an MTV email address. Suddenly we were in touch again. Every month or so we would write to each other. But as soon as I got excited, I wouldn't hear from him for a while. So Claudio got put on the back burner. I wasn't willing to work for what might end up being nothing, again.

Out of nowhere, I turned twenty-five. It seemed like a serious age to me. I looked at my life and started asking some hard questions: Where was the apartment I was supposed to have bought by now (it sounds like an absurd dream, but this was during the housing bubble, and people kept telling me to buy right away)? And the new car? Well, I did have a "new" car, but it was a forced gift that broke my budget when I had to replace the older car I'd crashed. Oops. It goes without saying that there was no room in my budget for a diamond.

All I'd been doing was working crazy hours and then rushing to "enjoy" my life in the little time I had to myself. It was a blur of traffic, getting ready for a night out, traffic again, standing in line to get into some new bar or club, traffic, a little sleep, traffic, followed by another long day at work. I realized I'd spent a good chunk of my life living it as if it were surgery: waiting for it to be over, confirming that everything had gone as planned, and recovering as quickly as possible so I'd be ready for what came next. There was nothing I did on my own for fun—everything was a production. I remember a colleague asking me what I did to relax, and I couldn't answer him. I used to like going to the movies, but I hadn't seen one in years. I liked to think I was an organized woman, but my room looked like a war zone. I considered myself an informed person, but I was not aware of current events—and I wasn't reading anything. I didn't own any of the music I liked. I was just on auto-pilot, busy by default.

The hardest thing was how all this distanced me from my family and friends. I was not around enough and I should have called more often. Sometimes, I couldn't even answer my own mom's calls because it was never "a good time to talk." I missed my friends' weddings (I don't care if they are divorced by now). Some friends spent weeks at the hospital and I was never able to visit them. I wrote my Christmas cards so late that they turned into New Year's cards (without a specific year in case they were really delayed) and had to rush back home right after my grandma's funeral because of work.

It wasn't just that I was busy. My professional life had started to feel, well, kind of empty. I had always been proud to work on artistic shows. Being part of TV and musical productions was a dream come true—some of my favorite credits are *Ricky Martin Unplugged, Santana Live From Mexico*, and the annual Latin Grammy Awards. There's nothing quite like the thrill of the lights, the audience applauding, the choreography, the live music. I loved sports shows, too, because the passion was overwhelming. People got real joy from those events, and I was happy to play some role. I took these kinds of jobs whenever I could, but the industry was shifting toward reality television, especially on music channels. It was hard to get excited about working on shows with pregnant teenage girls screaming at each other and scripts that enhanced fake drama. And the music itself? Enter reggaeton, dembow, trap, and twerking. I listened to the lyrics and got scared I was ruining a generation. Well, maybe that was a little dramatic, but that's what it felt like. When some friends from France came to visit with their two young daughters, we heard Pitbull's "El Taxi." One of the girls, a preteen, was singing in jumbled Spanish, *"Melocaló, El Taxi, Melocaló!"* I thought, thank God she isn't saying the actual lyrics, which are a euphemism for getting an erection, and then: I helped put that guy on stage a million times. It wasn't that I had somehow gained moral superiority. I didn't think I was better than anyone else. I was just personally uncomfortable with the work I was contributing to the world.

We were also in the middle of an economic crisis. Suddenly shows were being canceled, and freelancing became more and more risky. For the first time since my original job search six years earlier, I found myself looking for steady work. No one wanted to hire me. To this day, I have never been hired for a full-time job with benefits. Never. I guess people saw my resume and assumed that I was the freelancing type, out on my own so long that I was bound to leave for greener pastures. I interviewed for weeks and weeks, begging for jobs I didn't want and still feeling the sting of rejection. Ouch!

I finally got hired by one of the television networks where I used to freelance, but only on a technicality. I filled in for someone on maternity leave with a "permalancer" contract that was extended indefinitely. That was my longest experience with corporate red tape, sitting at a desk all day, and American office culture. Not exactly the glamorous work I'd imagined. Don't get me wrong: I loved my coworkers. I learned so much from my supervisor about how to delegate, organize my ideas, and manage other people. And she trusted me. My English wasn't that great at the time (still isn't!), but she knew I'd figure out what needed to be done, and that I wouldn't let her down. I did worry about the people I worked with in that office. Most of them were unhealthy—mentally and physically. Some of them used to cry in the bathroom at lunch, just like I did when I was having a bad day. One of our VPs actually had a heart attack in the office (he survived, thankfully). He was in his early fifties. I'll never forget watching the paramedics carry him out on a stretcher. It seemed sort of crazy that we were all putting ourselves through this stress in the name of award shows featuring twerking, semi-naked women, and the latest reality sensation.

I was feeling more and more conflicted every day. Then I went to a motivational workshop hosted by Alberto Sardiñas, a Venezuelan TV and radio personality. I took advantage of one of the exercises and asked anonymously what he would recommend to someone who wanted to be successful in the entertainment industry. I sat on the edge of my seat as he read my question. His answer: "My recommendation is to find out what your message is." His answer surprised me. What was my message? I had no idea.

Later, at the Billboard Latin Music Awards in Puerto Rico, I was sitting at a hip, poolside restaurant with my good friend, Melissa, and Daisy, a production veteran in her late sixties who was then the VP of Talent Development at a major Hispanic network in the US. This was possibly her last show before retirement. Melissa and I, in our youth and inexperience, were complaining to her about the impact of telenovelas and the stories they tell to society, especially to girls and women. We said we didn't want soap opera protagonists as role models. Daisy nodded in agreement. "I already did my part," she told us. "Now it's your turn."

I wanted to take her up on that challenge, but at the moment another life project was stealing focus: Claudio, *il professore*, who was newly off the back burner. He had visited me in Miami almost five years after we'd last seen each other. At first I didn't recognize him. His hair was shorter and reddish to my surprise. But he was as tall, skinny, and funny as I remembered. Driving home from the airport, we were both nervous. Claudio wouldn't stop staring at me. We kissed at the first light off the highway, and suddenly we were attempting to do an international long-distance relationship with different time zones and skyrocketing phone bills. I flew to Italy and we traveled the whole country together. When my friends saw the pictures, they said it looked like we were on our honeymoon. "Don't try too hard to be Superwoman," my friend Leana told me when she found out I was cooking and baking for Claudio—I had never cooked in my life, but had brought along my copy of *Mujer 2000*, a traditional Dominican cookbook that I'd figured might come in handy. Another friend encouraged me to go all out with her special recipe for chocolate mousse. They were constantly asking for updates.

We shared a brief but intense and extravagant six months of dating. We traveled, ate and drank, and took pictures of everything. It was full immersion, over the top. Sort of like *Eat Pray Love*, except in our case it was more like *Eat Play Love*. Then Claudio came back to Miami. We ate dinner one night at a waterfront hotel, and during dessert, I found a ring hiding in my chocolate cake. Forty-three people came to our wedding in Miami Beach a year later.

I still fantasize about the loft apartment we moved into on fashionable Brickell Avenue in downtown Miami. It was on the 20th floor with a gorgeous view of Biscayne Bay—sometimes we'd look down and see manatees—and featured a washer-dryer in our massive bathroom with double sinks and a stainless steel dishwasher. It felt sort of like we were dating as we explored Claudio's new city, trying out restaurants, going to Yngwie Malmsteen, Santana, Dave Matthews, and Metallica concerts, taking a weekend trip to Disney World or Cape Canaveral to sleep in the car and then witness the rocket launch being canceled. Claudio cooked amazing pasta, and sometimes we'd meet for lunch and warm up homemade lasagna in tin foil packets on the hood of the car. We loved to go out dancing. Any moment would become impromptu fun.

But we weren't exactly naturals at being married. We were still getting to know each other. In order to live in the same place, we'd had to get married, and I think we both felt rushed into it. You could say we had our fair share of disagreements: I liked white Christmas lights, he liked colored. We used to order Netflix DVDs (the original Netflix and chill), and Claudio would get upset because I'd fall asleep before the movie even started. Claudio, meanwhile, annoyed me with his tendency to become an expert in everything on his first try, even hurricanes, which he had never before experienced. We were both working jobs we disliked—Claudio had been demoted to the type of work he'd done eight years earlier, and for much less money—and speaking of money, we had to pay for the wedding and the expensive life we'd gotten ourselves into. We weren't alone, either. We saw a lot of empty apartments in downtown Miami due to the economic downturn; *la dolce vita* wasn't that dolce anymore. And there were more serious problems. Claudio had promised me on our honeymoon that he'd quit smoking cigarettes, but he left some ashes behind. I was immature and didn't know how to handle it, so I stopped talking to him for a week or two at a time (not a problem for me).

I would sit alone on the couch at night and stare out our floor-to-ceiling glass windows, wondering when everything changed. How did we end up like this? I was constantly reminded of a saying about marriage at the two-year mark: Do we plant a tree or sell the land?

Then my body gave me my first real red flag: an abnormal Pap smear. My doctor at Planned Parenthood confirmed that I had tested positive for HPV. They couldn't fit me in for a colposcopy for months, so I got online and found an office in North Miami Beach with the cheapest price (I had no insurance) and an opening that day. The results: CIN I, signaling slightly abnormal cells with mild dysplasia. I had cryosurgery the same day—I didn't want to waste one minute.

"Look how beautiful it looks," the gyn said to his assistant while peering inside me during the follow-up appointment. I got another Pap six months later. According to the doctor, I had "nothing to worry about," but considering that HPV can cause cervical cancer, I bought the best (and most expensive) health insurance coverage available, just in case. I couldn't disclose that I'd had these procedures or I would have been disqualified because of preexisting conditions. I took it as just another sign that things somehow had to change.

On the morning of my thirtieth birthday, I woke up alone on my younger sister Carla's couch, exactly eight blocks from our Brickell loft. I scanned my face, body, brain, and heart to see if I could sense any difference. Maturing, perhaps, or signs of aging. I looked in the mirror but found nothing.

Claudio and I had moved out of that beautiful apartment two days earlier. Neither of us had ever made such an organized move. We arranged glassware boxes, wardrobe boxes, and a giant U-Haul van. We put everything in storage except for one IKEA shelf I sold for $125. One of the security guards asked if we were getting divorced. I'd wanted to take a picture of the empty apartment, just as we did three years earlier when we moved in right before our wedding. Then we were young, we had bigger smiles. Three years later, our smiles were different—but we were in a rush. The picture we have from that day is of Claudio standing outside a storage unit with a single suitcase. Behind him, in the 10 x 25 jam-packed unit, is a black 2007 Honda Civic and everything else we owned.

My thirtieth birthday present to myself was a professional photo shoot with three wardrobe changes: professional, party, sexy. Those were my "looks" back then. I wanted to remember the best I could look at thirty. I'd carefully shopped for clothes and colorful accessories, and borrowed three pairs of shoes from my friend, Lumi—they were at least one size too big. I hadn't gone to this much trouble before in my life, even for my wedding. I'd asked the wedding photographer to photoshop my dark circles and crow's feet. This time I was fine with lines. When I got the CD with my pictures, I remember assessing my body, its shape and tone, all the marks on it. I thought I looked tired. Today, I see my beautiful black mane and a woman with so much energy.

After the photo shoot, it was time to celebrate. The sky was gray—I've had rain on almost all of my birthdays. I remember I wore white shorts and an asymmetrical tank top from Anthropologie that my friends Kris and Maruchi had given me as a gift. I picked up some popsicles and nachos at the neighborhood Publix and we partied in the daylight like children. A dozen more friends came later in the afternoon, jokingly asking when the clowns would arrive. The rain kept coming down. At night we drank mini bottles of liquor in Melissa's apartment. We were all trying to ignore the fact that this birthday party was also a reluctant goodbye. I would leave for Nicaragua in eleven days, and I didn't know when I was coming back.

Claudio's big break had come: a new job as Master Blender and Director of Operations at Mombacho Cigars. He would be based in Nicaragua, and I was going with him. I chose love over steady work, and being with my husband over coming home to an empty apartment, even a loft with a private washer-dryer and that stunning view. We had decided to take the leap—together. It would be a chance to start again, and I think we both knew that's what we needed.

Every woman I know has told me some version of this same story. We come from all kinds of families—loving, difficult, complicated. We fall in love like crazy, but it's a lot harder than we thought. We travel the world, we move to new cities and countries. We start careers. We adapt and adjust. We're told that thirty is a major milestone. But I turned thirty without having what I "must" have, without having done what I "must" do. At thirty, I was uncertain about everything in my life.

But it felt more like a beginning than an ending. It was a clean slate: take three. I wasn't afraid so much as confused. Did thirty have to be so filled with pressure and expectations? Why couldn't our thirties be positive and even fun? Some of my friends had turned thirty, and I was honored to be part of their celebrations: driving convertibles through the desert outside of Las Vegas, enjoying surprise Mariachi serenades at sport bars, hiring John Mayer impersonators for home parties, eating *pastelitos* and *croquetas* at a Cuban quinceañera-themed office party. Later on I met a woman who decided to move to New York on her thirtieth birthday, another who climbed Kilimanjaro to raise funds for the hospital that saved her from cancer at age six, and another who took the year off from her real estate career to learn how to sew, work at an antique store, and take ballet classes.

I wanted to know what women and men were thinking, feeling, and doing at this age. I wanted to hear everyone's story. And I wanted to get my own story straight. After the photo shoot, after another move to another country and culture—what was I really going to do with this decade?

Five months before my birthday, I started writing a "document." I didn't know how long it was going to be. I didn't mind if it was a diary, a Facebook post, a magazine article, or a book. I wanted to put in writing and share what I was experiencing. And I was looking for answers. I invited old and new friends to express their thoughts, feelings, experiences, jokes, realizations, epiphanies, and complaints about turning thirty and being a thirty-something—that way we all got to vent, and share. A month later, the "document" became a blog. And a month shy of my birthday, the document and blog became this book, with life as an ever-generous and sometimes confusing muse.

Once I got to Nicaragua, I sat down and started typing with the speed of a talented pianist. But then I started to realize how hard it is to write a book. I am not a natural writer and English is my second language. Distractions came in many shapes and forms, from mosquitoes to hormones to Claudio slaving away in the kitchen while I tried to finish my word count for the day. Each birthday became a reminder of this big pending project and my failure to complete it. I spent four years cemented to a chair, leaving everything else I wanted to do for later. I asked myself: Why can't I just finish it? Who am I to write a book anyway? Then I realized what the problem was: I was just a few years into my thirties. I was trying to write about something I hadn't yet lived. So I decided it was time to break up with my outline and enjoy life instead. I needed to just be in my thirties, to explore them and then report back.

This book is a time capsule. I wrote it between the ages of twenty-nine and thirty-seven. The final draft is very different from the first. It still asks the same questions, but it does so with a bit more wisdom (I hope), and a lot more life experience. These years have left their mark on me, and on everyone else in the book. The experts in Part Two evolved, as did their messages and platforms. The guest contributors in Part Four sent me their reflections throughout the process. Since then, some have gotten married, some have gotten divorced. Babies were born and not born. Four of the women were diagnosed with cancer. Only two survived. When writing was difficult for me, I told myself I owed it to these women to publish their words as I had promised.

What follows is a labor of love—emphasis on labor. In Part Two, I share my interviews with an accomplished group of expert contributors on the following topics: People, Health, Spirit, Work, Money, and Living. Part Three is the story of my thirties so far, and what I know now , or what I feel now, at age thirty-seven. Part Four is a compilation of more than fifty essays written by friends from around the world.

I hope what you find here inspires you. I hope the stories comfort you and make you laugh. I hope you find strategies and ideas that can help you make the most of this challenging and transformative decade. I am not trying to persuade you in any way—I am simply telling my story, and I hope it inspires you to tell yours.

II

What Matters Most

PEOPLE | HEALTH | SPIRIT | WORK | MONEY | LIVING

- *People* -

"TO LOVE ONESELF IS THE BEGINNING OF
A LIFELONG ROMANCE."
Oscar Wilde

———

"PEOPLE ARE ALWAYS THE MOST IMPORTANT."
Rhyna, my landlord, roommate, and foster mom

In March 2007, I was standing on the red carpet at the elegant National Theater in Santo Domingo for Premios Casandra, an annual awards show that celebrates Dominican art and culture. After weeks of long, exhausting pre-production days, show day had finally arrived. No, I wasn't in the designer dress of my dreams. I was wearing all black to make myself invisible, as was mandatory for production workers, with my greasy hair pulled into a high bun and my headset tangled in my earrings from walking dozens of singers and comedians to the live interview set. Television production is always hectic, but there was some extra drama that night. A jealous producer wanted to sabotage the event, and sent four strange men who arrived in a limo wearing only their underwear. I screamed as they stepped onto the red carpet. Luckily, security jumped on top of them just before they reached the cameras. Crisis averted. My friend, Heidi, was in the trenches with me that night as one of our talent escorts, the production employees who accompanied artists to key camera spots before leading them to their seats. In spite of our efforts to hide off screen, the cameras kept catching us as we waited for talent and rushed them through their "walk of fame."

When it was all over, my cell phone rang at the exact same moment as Heidi's. My mom and sister had called to congratulate me because they knew how hard I had worked. "You looked like a celebrity walking up and down the carpet!" Carla said. "You rocked that bun like a star! *De aquí pa' Hollywood!*" Even though I didn't believe her and regretted being caught on camera—a classic production mistake—she put a smile on my face, and I laughed maybe for the first time that day. Heidi's mother had called for a different reason. "If you knew you were going to be on camera, why didn't you dress better?" she asked. "Why were you running around like that? You should have fixed your hair, done your make-up, and worn something nicer. You looked crazy."

In that moment I understood how much the people and relationships around us contribute to our reality and self-worth—especially when it comes to our parents. I was so proud of my work on that show and where my career was headed, but my friend was crushed, despite meeting and taking a picture with her idol that night (another production mistake). Even now I can see the consequences of Heidi's upbringing. She's still finding her own strength, still on a journey to understand herself, like all of us.

Years later, when a Cuban mechanic was fixing my broken down car in Miami, he mentioned that he'd been married for thirty years. I asked him, "What's the secret?"

"Before you get married, you really have to know your in-laws," he told me. "Because they are the models that your partner will always see and try to replicate (or avoid to the extreme). Make sure you're okay with that." He confirmed what I had seen all along with my friends and their parental models. I guess that's why I consider my friends some of my greatest teachers—they showed me how our personalities are shaped, and they helped me understand the consequences of how you treat other people. From them I was able to choose the best practices and try to apply them to my life. I didn't always get it right—not even close—but at least I had a sense of the right direction.

My own parents imparted so much wisdom—my father's clarity, grace, thoughtfulness, spontaneity, self-love; my mother's strength, discretion, honesty, transparency, humility. Both of my parents are a source of comfort for me, even now. I will never outgrow taking naps with my mom. She is the only adult other than my husband that I can cuddle with and not feel awkward. They also showed me what it is to suffer, and what it looks like when you come through on the other side. My dad was forced to leave the family and the country for safety during local political turmoil, and we ended up merging with my aunt, who was facing her own struggles. As I got older, I had to look outside our blended family to learn more about how the world worked. But I have nothing but respect for how I was raised to be a strong woman with traditional values, how I never felt the emotional and financial pressures my family constantly faced. "Honor thy father and thy mother" is not only a commandment but also the noblest act of gratitude. I've seen people repair their relationships with their parents by starting from a place of respect and gratitude, knowing that their mom and dad did the best they could with the knowledge they had. This is even more important in our thirties and beyond, as our parents start to decline in health and strength.

Another piece of advice that clarified relationships for me: Rhyna, my mom's friend who hosted me when I first arrived in Miami, always used to say: "People are the most important." That struck me at the time and still does. In any situation, protect the person. Not your new shoes that may have been ruined, not your manicured nails, not your own expectations and disappointments. People are the most important. That simple phrase has stopped me in so many heated moments from doing or saying something truly regrettable.

And then there's my relationship with myself, which dictates the people I surround myself with, how I take care of my health, what I do with my time in this world, the way I live, the work I prefer, how I spend my money, and, above all, what I believe and portray about who I really am. A lot of people struggle with this relationship the most. I struggled, too, when I was younger, especially when it came to my frizzy hair, hairy legs, and even my skin color. But with the strong support I had at home, I learned how to love myself. Now I make a point of trying to feel and look good (no matter my budget), whether it's homemade natural beauty treatments, aerobics sessions, or my favorite magazines. When I want something, I go for it. Somehow I'm confident despite the fact that I've failed plenty of times.

It's my relationship with my husband where I still feel like a work-in-progress. In the same way that I have learned to accept the partners that my loved ones choose, I am learning to accept my own relationship. I was not trained for marriage, and ten years later, I am still in training. At some point I declared myself incompetent. I surrendered. And then it became easier. When I was single, I firmly believed that I was a reasonable person, but I learned (sometimes the hard way) that I had more than a few flaws: my heart was calloused, I was full of doubts, and I lacked trust, all of which made me not exactly who I wanted to be as a wife. Previous direct and indirect experiences had coded me incorrectly. I had to undo all of that. I had to stop hovering in order to be the woman, wife, professional, and happy person that I actually am. And I got to know myself better through my actions and reactions to the new challenges I faced: being in a partnership helped me discover many unknown parts of myself.

In my thirties, I have a much broader concept of what relationships and love really mean. Now the most important questions are:

Am I doing my best?

How am I contributing to the success of my relationships? Of my people?

How can I be a better spouse, a better community member, and a better person?

Am I assuming my responsibilities with goodwill and humility?

Am I promoting respect and consideration?

Am I a source of love?

Joy?

Peace?

Kindness?

Understanding?

Wisdom?

Personal relationships are the foundation, and from that comes community, which we all help shape and which we all need to avoid depression, addiction, isolation, illness, and so many other problems. Today, I try to give back in every little interaction because I know that a simple gesture such as eye contact can make a big difference in loved ones and in strangers. Relationships fuel our lives, for better or worse, but people are always the most important.

I'm now raising a little boy who will someday become a man. He has reminded me that love is energy. It's what keeps me going. I run on love. So does Luca. He is my focus, and he is the future.

Of all the relationships we invest in, our relationships with ourselves should be the healthy base upon which we build everything else. There are multiple ways to explore this "life-long romance," as Wilde says. Autumn Whitefield-Madrano, an author and feminist beauty expert, sees self-love as a powerful kind of beauty:

When I was a kid, my mother didn't wear makeup at all—maybe mascara, but nothing else. But whenever I visited my grandmother, I would sit at her makeup table and play for hours. I loved trying on different lipsticks and eye shadows. It was just this world of fantasy that I loved engaging in, but I didn't know how to do it because I didn't learn firsthand from my mom. So when I started working in women's magazines in my early twenties, even though I wasn't in the beauty department, my heart was there—I always loved the beauty pages, and I loved talking to beauty editors. Beauty is literally the face that we present to the world. I am more surprised when people are not interested in beauty. You are interested in beauty in some way even if you don't wear makeup. It's what you are showing the world, and that says so much about who you are.

That is how I got attracted to the subject of beauty, and I've engaged with it for as long as I can remember. Now I am a beauty blogger, but I don't write about makeup tips—I look at why we are invested in beauty as women and the role that it plays in our lives. I started The Beheld when I was thirty-four. Therefore, I had some sense of what I wanted out of life in terms of who I was, and that enabled me to start this blog in the first place.

Most women become more comfortable with who they are as they get older, and that shows in the way they present themselves. The way they do their makeup or don't do their makeup, the way they style their hair or the clothes they wear. When I was younger I was a lot more experimental. I wouldn't even leave the house without wearing wild eye shadow—I was playing around. But there wasn't a sense of joy in it, it was almost a search for identity: Who am I? Am I someone who wears bright red lipstick? Am I someone who has short hair? Do I have long hair? Do I have highlights? I was trying to define my identity by who I was physically, and we all do that. As we get older we understand the variety of identities available to us, so instead of searching for "Oh! That's my one identity!" you understand that sometimes you want to wear your natural curls and other times you want your hair sleek, and I am the same way. I go through phases when I want to wear my hair long and luxurious and puffed out—and other times, like during the summer, I just twist it up with a pencil and that's it. I understand that there are different faces I am showing to the world. I am not looking for my identity: I am presenting various sides of myself.

My approach has become a little narrower in a certain sense, now that I know what works for me. But I didn't know that fifteen years ago. I didn't understand what my features were, what I should be emphasizing. We learn with time. Some ladies have a knack for it when they're younger, but I was certainly not one of them. I have also become more comfortable with what I do have to offer and learned to trust those things that are worth showing off. I never thought like that when I was a teenager. I knew I had nice big hazel eyes but I was afraid to show them off because I thought I might seem arrogant if I tried to emphasize them with eyeliner. As I get older, I tell myself: Everyone has things about themselves that they know are beautiful and they should show them off.

I spent so much time as a teenager thinking I had bad skin because of some pimples. Yes, I had pimples, but I had elastic, smooth skin, except for those occasional pimples, and I wish I had been able to recognize that as "good skin" instead of always saying "bad skin," because it was just teenage girl skin.

Something that helped me in my early thirties was looking at old pictures of myself and seeing how nice I looked. I was never one of those stunningly beautiful women, but in my college pictures I just had this glow. My hair was shining and bouncy and healthy. I didn't know how to dress myself, but I had gifts that I didn't let myself believe in when I was younger, and it dawned on me: That means there are still things within myself that I don't know, there's still something lovely, there's always going to be something lovely even if I don't recognize it right now. I have to trust that it's there. I try to remember that when I have a bad day. Whatever I saw yesterday and liked is still there, and in ten years I'm going to look back at a picture of myself now and wonder why I didn't see some other quality.

One of the biggest things that helped me make peace and make friends with my image was understanding that when I looked in the mirror, I wasn't seeing how I looked—I was seeing how I felt. Once I realized that, I didn't take the mirror as the final truth. I still sometimes wake up with puffy skin or my hair just isn't working, but as long as we take care of ourselves and get enough rest, we look the same most of the time. The biggest problem I see with women in their thirties, who are now a little more comfortable with themselves, isn't so much that they don't like what they see or that they think they are hideous—it's that their self-esteem fluctuates a lot. One day they might feel like, "Hello, I'm Miss Thing," but the next day they feel terrible. I would like to see women have more trust in those days when they like what they see in the mirror, or not need to look in the mirror at all. It's about having a certain faith in what you are showing the world. On the days when we see something we don't like, more often than not, it's about mood or something internal—it's not about, "Oh, my eyes look smaller today than usual," because your eyes do not get smaller, I promise.

Some people think that if they are unhappy, they need to mask it somehow. I don't think that is the best way for beauty to relate to our happiness. First of all, there is no evidence that beautiful people are happier. There are statistics about how conventionally attractive people earn more money—more so for men than for women, but that is another story. These people might be seen as more competent or more likable, but there is no evidence that they are happier. Science has shown that we get happier as we get older, which is contrary to what some people think. I'd like to apply the same idea to beauty, recognizing that most people look how they feel on a day-to-day basis, and they often feel better as they age—so they will also look better. I would like to see women trust their instincts more and draw on their real life experience instead of looking at media and advertising messages about youth being something that we need to cling to. Real, lived experience shows the genuine connection between our own form of beauty and our happiness.

As women get older, they have more trust in what they have to offer on a purely physical level—the more they learn to highlight that, the better they feel. Though makeup can still be used to help shift our mindsets. For instance, putting on lipstick might transform the way you look at yourself. I remember talking to an Iraqi war veteran about how she learned to apply camouflage makeup in the army, and when she looked in the mirror she recognized herself as a soldier. It changed the way she viewed herself and now she applies that insight to wearing makeup in her daily life. When we put on our face, our "war paint," we can all transform. That could be something joyous for women to experiment with.

I'm especially interested in the concept of mature beauty in women around the world and from many different walks of life. I haven't interviewed women from France yet, but just from talking with French women, I've learned that the age range in which women in the media are considered beautiful is much broader. There is a scene in *Eat Pray Love*, Elizabeth Gilbert's memoir, where she goes to Italy in her late thirties and is surprised that men aren't chasing her down the street like they did when she was twenty. And a local says, "It's not like France, where they dig the old babes." In French movies mature women play the leads and they are seen as beautiful and sensual. That is happening more in America, but we have a ways to go. Other cultures have a stronger holistic view of beauty. Many Asian cultures revere the elderly—for them it is a given that you would take in your parents and your grandparents as they age. There's an automatic respect for the wisdom you accumulate over a lifetime. We don't understand that yet in our culture; we understand it intellectually, but we don't value aging that way. At least our generation doesn't.

Changing roles in our society have been wonderful for women, for the most part. Our grandmothers could only be housewives and mothers, or maybe they could be career women, but then they couldn't have children. Women from our generation have many more options, which is liberating but also overwhelming. As America and the West in general become more comfortable with the variety of roles women can play, I hope we will be able to opt-in and opt-out of beauty, with beauty seen as just one of many roles. I'm not trying to say that Asian cultures are doing that already, but there is more understanding of what a sixty-five-year-old woman has to offer to the world and to younger generations. Once we get closer to that understanding, we'll be closer to a holistic concept of beauty.

We are the first generation that has had the opportunity to see women we considered starlets in our twenties grow into the stars they are today. Julia Roberts is still on magazine covers after age fifty. Helen Hunt is in her mid-fifties. Julianne Moore, a mature woman who is still seen beautiful, is fifty-nine. Rue McClanahan was fifty-two when she was cast in *The Golden Girls*. McClanahan was a beautiful woman but she was seen as a senior citizen—meanwhile, Julianne Moore is a sex symbol! But this begs the question: At what age can women stop trying to be seen as beautiful? That's another discussion, as is understanding that women over twenty-five are sexual creatures.

There is no magic bullet to achieving beauty. If you eat healthy foods, exercise, get enough sleep, drink a lot of water, don't smoke, and don't drink much alcohol, that will show up in the way you look. You can dye your hair if it starts to go gray, but there is no way to fake the natural glow that comes from taking care of yourself. I certainly did not understand that in my twenties, not at all. I thought advice telling us to take care of ourselves was a trick to get us to do healthy things—I felt fine no matter what I did in my twenties. Now, the difference is remarkable. If I've got a heavy work schedule and can't get to the gym for a few weeks, I can tell in my energy, and I can tell in my face. It's not that I look ugly. It's that I don't have the natural glow that comes from doing everything I should be doing. Women at our age understand this a lot more.

There are certain things you can do, like using retinoid cream, which is the only product proven to work on fine lines and wrinkles. It's a bit expensive, but it lasts for months and I have seen a difference in my skin. I wasn't great at eating a lot of vegetables—I just don't have the time to sit down and eat twelve ounces of greens, so I have a green smoothie almost every morning. I eat other vegetables throughout the day as well, but if I don't have a chance, the smoothie takes care of it. That's my biggest trick: the green smoothie. As far as muscle loss, I've been going to the gym regularly for ten years, but I only started seriously strength training a few years ago, and I feel amazing. I can tell the difference in my body. I don't want to say I look younger, because I don't, but I look better than I did five years ago, even though I look five years older. I see a lot of women in the gym spending so much time on the treadmill. Running is good for you, but only up until a certain point. If you want to boost your metabolism, you have to strength train. It's been a wonderful journey for me. I wish more women weren't afraid to pick up heavy weights—you are not going to get big and bulky. I lift the heaviest weights I can, but I haven't turned into the Hulk.

Understand your features. If you are insecure or genuinely unsure, there are makeup artists that can help you identify your best attributes. Most women in their thirties know what their gifts are. We all have days when we look in the mirror and feel amazing. I see this more and more as we age, and I want more women to embrace what is striking, unusual, and sexy about them. This sounds cliché, but it's true: Confidence is attractive. Confidence is sexy, and there are no shortcuts. Meditation can help you feel calm and confident when you're struggling. I can't say that it directly translates, that when I'm meditating every day, or as often as I can, I'm more beautiful—it doesn't work like that. But we live incredibly stressful lives, and stress does show up in our faces and our bodies. Doing whatever you can to find some peace is very helpful. In my case, exercise, meditation, and recognizing my need for alone time are key. I am friendly, but essentially I am very introverted. I wish I had recognized that when I was younger.

No one is going to think you are more beautiful than you believe you are at your best. Of course everyone looks at us and sees something different, and we have no way of controlling that, but as long as there is some part of you that believes you have something special to offer, people will recognize it and respond. You don't always have to feel it, but learning how to access that can be a great gift.

I was at a baby shower a few years ago where I was one of the mother-to-be's oldest friends, and she was the oldest of her friends. It was interesting to be there with a group of twenty-three-year-olds. We were talking about age and I mentioned mine—I was thirty-seven then—and these women turned around and asked: "You're thirty-seven? But you look so good!" And I said: "Thank you!" But I don't look better or younger than any of my friends who are in the same age group; we know that you have to take care of yourself. When you are young, you have this notion of what being thirty-something or forty-something looks like, and that's an outdated idea. Those twenty-three-year-olds will find out in fifteen years that being thirty-seven doesn't mean you are writing yourself off—it's the beginning in a lot of ways.

I want those younger women to read this. I want them to see what we have done with our lives and that there is so much to look forward to. That sentiment is out there and growing, but you still find women who think thirty is old… Oh Gosh, not thirty! When I was twenty-three, I couldn't wait to be in my thirties. I was so excited to turn thirty, and whenever I hear women say the same, I smile and think: Right on!

AUTUMN WHITEFIELD-MADRANO is the author of *Face Value: The Hidden Ways Beauty Shapes Women's Lives* (Simon & Schuster, 2016). Her writing has appeared in *Marie Claire, Glamour, Salon, Jezebel, The Guardian,* and more. She created The Beheld, a blog examining questions behind personal appearance. Her work on the ways beauty shapes women's lives has been covered by *The New York Times* and the *Today* show. She lives in Astoria, Queens, and will tell you her beauty secrets if you tell her yours.

Sexual relationships are essential and pleasurable but also confusing and complicated. In order to explore sexuality in our thirties and how to better communicate our needs, I asked Jill Di Donato, lifestyle writer and editor, to share her expertise:

Here's a fun anecdote for you. Let's call it, "In Defense of Snooping." I was seeing this guy a couple years back. We'd only gone on a few dates and had made out, but I was at his place, and figured tonight was "the night." The guy leaves me in his room while he goes into the kitchen and prepares some beverages and a tray of snacks (we had a whole night of "movie watching" planned). While he was gone, I took the opportunity to "look around," a term commonly referred to as snooping. Why women do this is beyond me—what do we hope to find? Pictures of exes, diaries about how they feel about us (do men even keep diaries?), a ginormous pile of dirty socks? In any event, what I found was a prescription bottle of pills with my date's name on them. One quick search on my smartphone, and I discovered said pills were to treat outbreaks of an STD that stays with you for life. I was horrified, told him I wasn't feeling well, and never spoke to him again. You may consider this rash, but I wasn't in the market to date someone who could give me a disease.

Anecdote number two: I call this one, "Women Aren't The Only Ones With Ticking Clocks." I was dating this guy who happened to be a bit younger than me. We were still casual, but sleeping together, when one night, he said to me, "You're getting a little old to not consider having a baby. I'd make a great dad." I ordered another tequila shot and replied, "Aren't we going to a Black Keys show tonight?" The next couple times we were in bed, the guy was persistent about having unprotected sex. But I wasn't keen on him being my baby daddy, so I came up with excuses like, "I have my period," to get out of it. When he said he knew I didn't have my period because he was familiar with my cycle, it was time to get the heck out. My friend Rick wasn't reassuring: "I know guys who've poked holes in condoms to get a girl pregnant." Fast-forward seven months later, and this guy is indeed a father-to-be, having gotten another woman pregnant right around the time we stopped seeing each other. Of course, I don't know the details of the pregnancy, but let's just say I'm thankful that I won't be giving up tequila anytime soon.

Anecdote number three: "Under Pressure." A successful, gorgeous friend of mine confessed to me that in her twenties, she was much more of a prude. But now that she's in her thirties and with more experience under her belt, she says she has sex much more frequently. Sometimes, it's because her libido calls for a dash of passion, but sometimes, she explains, "It's just easier to give in to a guy pressuring me than to have some awkward confrontation with someone you actually like. I don't want to turn him off." I would expect this reaction from a less-experienced woman.

My friend is having what I'll call "strategic sex." Even though she'll participate in "strategic sex" every so often, she's not so much a fan of this type of encounter. "If I don't know the guy that well, I'm not comfortable with him giving me oral sex because you can't use protection for that. So, the least he can do is supply lube, because if she's not completely into it, a dry condom isn't fun for a woman." While my friend is having safe physical sex, and even though she's completely cognizant of the fact that a guy who pressures her into sex is likely not "the one," she admits she usually feels "taken advantage of," especially if the guy doesn't call or act as interested after she's slept with him. Her "strategy" is to weed out the players and guys just interested in sex, but I wonder, even though she is no naïf in the bedroom and understands that it requires strategies, is her form of self-protection really serving her needs?

I call anecdote number four "Coming Clean" (no pun intended). A friend in show business is dating a guy she really likes, but they haven't been dating for that long. He disclosed to her that he has an STD and they have not yet slept together. "He earned major points with me for this," she tells me. "But what do I do?" she wants to know. "Do I continue to see him?" Okay—first, has dating become so jaded that being honest about physical conditions that can and will affect a partner's well-being is considered something to earn "major points" for? I shudder at the thought. Second, it's too early in my friend's relationship for her to know if she wants to be monogamous with her guy, but she said she'd consider taking preventative measures (i.e., drugs that can ward off the STD) if he were to commit to her. It's my firm belief that monogamy is an elective choice, and that two people should enter into it because it's a burning desire, not to prevent a burning down there. But my friend's dilemma got me thinking: Even when we take all physical measures to protect ourselves in sexual relationships, are we ever really safe? And now that we're in our thirties, the decade where women can and should be taking all preventative measures to maintain a safe body for the future (we have more knowledge about resources available to us; we've most likely had a sex-related health scare and have dealt with it accordingly; we can be proactive about taking extra good care of our bodies with regular doctor check-in's and mind-body exercises), we're also deciding whether we plan to reproduce or not.

Despite my opening horror stories, safety is not only possible, but it should be every thirty-something woman's bottom line. But by no means does that mean safety is boring. I have a married friend who says that feeling safe with her husband is a complete and utter turn on. "Oh, I've had some wild times with really hot guys," she tells me (and as she is one of New York's former "It Girls," I believe her). "But what I love about my husband, who is the hottest man on the planet to me, is that he makes me feel 100 percent safe all the time. It's the most amazing feeling."

I'm sure there may be an evolutionary reason or two that a woman is hardwired to want to feel safe, but given the dating horror stories above, it also seems like common sense. When we hop into bed with someone, things change. This is a departure for me—a revelation I've come to as of late: A handshake is casual, a nod is casual. Sex is anything but. The truth is, after sex, I do feel more vulnerable with a man, and not hearing from him will sting a hundred times more than if we hadn't slept together. So, I've started doing these odd ritualistic things to protect myself before I even enter into a sexual relationship with a man:

1. I won't ever talk about him to my parents. (This seems like the kiss of death. For real. Every time I mention a guy to my parents, he stops calling or I get a text like, "Sorry I've been so busy lately." It takes less than a minute to shoot a "thinking of you" text.)

2. I take his text messages at face value and won't spend one minute analyzing them with my friends.

3. I put him in my phone under a code name.

Do these things keep me safe? Probably not. But they give me an illusion of control in the world of dating where sometimes you can feel like you're never safe from the blows of rejection, humiliation, frightening doctor's visits, loneliness, and delusion (i.e. OMG I must be a total troll because he hasn't texted after our amazing date!) But all is not lost. I think the key to feeling safe is to act in a self-protective way and read the signs a guy throws at you correctly, and then, ahem, act upon them (I know that's the hard part). So, here are four signs that you might be entering an unsafe romantic relationship:

1. *You feel slightly manipulated.* Men, especially those in high-powered or creative jobs, are manipulative by nature. You can't sell corporate accounts, book an acting job, or raise venture capital without being able to manipulate people. It's just the way of the world. And manipulation doesn't always have to be a negative thing in the work world. But in relationships, it is not so good. Sometimes, it takes me a while to realize that I've been manipulated. I try to make excuses for the manipulative behavior. The best thing to do, however, is get out before you end up being manipulated into something that can irrevocably change your life.

2. *He is erratic in his pursuit of you.* I'm all for women making the first move, or even the second. But if your guy lays it on thick and then begins to withhold his attention for you, something isn't right. He should be trying to make you feel safe and wanted, not confused.

3. *He talks about the future, but doesn't follow up on plans, set dates, or give you a solid sense of security.* Enough said.

4. If on your first few dates, rather than sharing past stories, memories, or even former relationship talk in an attempt to build safety by creating genuine intimacy, *he brings up his ex, financial instability, or how stressful and busy his life is*, he is not making a concerted effort to make you feel safe. It may not be conscious on his part or even mean he's a jerk, but it's an excellent indication of how he will prioritize your needs for safety inside and outside of the bedroom.

Once and only once we are safe in a relationship, (Okay, I'm speaking for me, and relationship has myriad meanings) can I truly enjoy the sex. Oh, and did I mention I'm in the decade where my sexuality is at its peak? For years women in their thirties have been told that this is the decade when we're going to have mind-blowing, multi-orgasmic, hair-pulling sex. I, as a woman in my thirties, think that's tremendous pressure (and not the good kind) to face between the sheets. The ever-wise Dr. Ruth, who in her early nineties still gives stellar sex advice, says, "I question all such theories about peaks. I think that such phenomena are individual."

So rather than focusing on reports and statistics and the quantification of pleasure, I will pause to talk a little about my own experience. I have learned that sex is much more pleasurable in my thirties. In your twenties, sex is fine, but not as passionate because you're still trying to figure things out. Getting to know yourself physically and emotionally makes for better sex. Learning what love is makes for better sex. Caring about others makes for better sex. You're also probably having sex with more experienced partners, so you have learned a thing or two.

In my twenties sex was more physical—I was more consumed with some idealized "feeling" I thought being sexual was all about. Sure, that was a step up from teen sex, which was just a disaster, but there was still plenty of progress to be made. Now that I'm in my thirties, sex is more holistic—it can incorporate a mental, spiritual, and psychodynamic connection with my partner, while still sending chills down my spine. Complexity makes for better sex, and women in our thirties are complex, beautiful creatures.

If mind-blowing, multi-orgasmic, hair-pulling sex is what you're after, here are eight things I've learned about sex now that I'm in my thirties:

1. *Experiment with the rolling O.* Although this isn't actually scientifically proven, a girlfriend of mine swears by what she calls the "rolling O." What you do is hold your breath during the moments building up to and during your climax for an intensified, extended orgasm. I've tried it, and although it requires a little concentration at first, practice pays off, and with the "rolling O" you have greater control over your pleasure.

2. *Know and accept your body.* As a woman in your thirties, you should definitely be familiar with your vagina, what feels like what and how everything works. If you're worrying about things like taste, smell, or sounds, you're detracting from the physical sensations of pleasure. Being comfortable with yourself pays off, too: When you're less inhibited not only will you feel sexier, your partner will experience more enjoyment. Says a friend, "I like that I don't always feel like I have to cater to the guy like when I was younger. I feel now I can let go and not have to be perfect." P.S. Part of accepting our bodies is primal humanity. We're animals, and that's sexy. Also, having a *c'est la vie* attitude about a funny situation in bed shows a man that sex doesn't always have to be this "serious thing"–that we're doing it for pleasure and fun.

3. *Get comfortable with certain skills.* Women in their thirties are known for several things among my younger set of male pals: their confidence, careers, and superior skills when it comes to oral sex. By now, oral sex is hopefully something you enjoy, and if you're like me, the more you enjoy something, the better you are at it. Share tips with your female friends, guy friends, and gay friends of both genders, but more than that, learn how to communicate with your partner. Try a couple of different techniques and ask what he or she likes best.

Personally, on the receiving side, I've found that men in their thirties (as opposed to younger men) are better at it. My thirty+ male friend admits, "Honestly, it takes years to perfect the skills. I've learned what works and what doesn't. My advice to those who want to please a woman this way: listen to her. She doesn't have to say anything verbally–her body language speaks for itself. How she reacts, quivers, moans–all of these give you cues on how to proceed."

4. *Be comfortable setting your own boundaries.* Just like a thirty-year-old woman doesn't kowtow to the latest trends in fashion, she sets her own style bar when it comes to sex. Some things, like BDSM, might not be for you, but that doesn't make you "vanilla." If missionary gets you off, go for it! By now, you know yourself and what you're comfortable with. Own it. On the other hand, if you feel like being adventurous, there's no age limit on expanding your horizons.

5. *Know what you want before you sleep with someone.* If a relationship is what you covet, don't waste your time with one-night stands. You might think these carnal flings are meaningless, but the excitement they give you is like a drug–and gives you a rush. Like any high, the roller coaster of emotions (you're self-inflicting) is keeping you from pursuing a solid connection with a partner. Likewise, if commitment isn't your thing, don't force a relationship because it's what you think you "ought" to be doing. You make the rules. Along these lines, by your thirties, you have enough experience to discern what others

want out of you, so your Pollyanna days are done. Trust your instincts about people; listen to yourself.

6. *Get ready for more connected sex.* I've found that something switched in me now that I'm older—it could be all the things listed in this piece: my confidence, control, greater love for myself and my body, or it could be that I've finally fit into my skin. This translates into sex where you are fully connected to your partner, in sync, and reaching towards being fully intimate. It can be powerful, and has left me in tears several times (which can freak a guy out, so be sure to explain these are tears of sexual passion). A lot of people suffer in relationships because they're trying to hold on too tight to their partner or they're not able to open themselves up enough. A successful relationship is about being able to stand alone, as well as with your partner. Now that I'm able to stand on my own, sexually, I neither hold on too tight nor close myself off.

7. *Your "list" is for your eyes only.* Now that you're in your thirties, and, if like me, single, chances are you've racked up a certain number. Recently, I made "the list." Some of the names on the list brought me fond memories; others made me cringe. Being aware of your sexual past will help you fine-tune what you're looking for—and what you're not. By no means share the list with a lover or even a friend. It's for you and you alone.

8. *Own your sex life.* Whether that means dealing with the fact that you've had a one-night stand (washing your sheets and moving on) or that you are completely blown away each time you make love to your partner, admit, at least to yourself, what you're really feeling. Naïf no longer, you are a woman who has a certain *joie de vivre,* and this includes your sex life. Be broad with what sexuality means—you've earned the right to have it mean many things. Maybe you are in an amazing monogamous sexual relationship and are over the moon; maybe you're debating between multiple lovers for their variety of skillsets; maybe you enjoy yourself—because you are fabulous, and just because you don't have a man in your bed doesn't mean you're not a sexual being. If this is the case, indulge your sexual self in other ways: get a massage and let your body be pampered, and take this time to care for your body—exfoliate it, moisturize it, experiment with scents, wear lingerie, sleep naked with the window open and feel the breeze on your skin; explore yourself.

—— **JILL DI DONATO** is a lifestyle writer and editor with over fifteen years experience. She holds a BA from Barnard College and an MFA from Columbia University. Her first novel *Beautiful Garbage* was published by She Writes Press in 2013 and produced as a short film. As a journalist, she's covered celebrity news, politics, and style. Her personal essays take up issues of gender, relationships, fashion, art, education, and feminism.

Currently, she's a contributing writer for *Modern Luxury* and most recently, she was the founding fashion and beauty editor at *Culture Trip*. Bylines include *VICE, Los Angeles Times, Salon, Autre, Refinery29, Bustle, MilK, NYLON, Tin House, Electric Literature, and Glamour.* For five years, she wrote a sex column at the Huffington Post.

Health

In the winter of 2012, six months after my initial HPV scare when I was told there was "nothing to worry about," I had another Pap. It came back abnormal again. This time the test showed CIN III—severely abnormal cells—which meant I needed a LEEP[1] procedure in order to electrosurgically remove the abnormal tissue. I visited a total of three doctors, went through four tests and three procedures, including one that left me at risk of future miscarriage, endured eight weeks of no sexual intercourse, no swimming pools, and no tampons, and not one doctor offered advice for how I could prevent this from happening again. None of them suggested any changes in my lifestyle or diet. After my many questions, one doctor finally said: "If you want, you can take folic acid, and condoms help, too." That's it. Off to the next patient. Even worse, when I received the summary of charges from my insurance company, I saw that they had coded CIN III as "Stage 1 Cancer." The doctors didn't tell me that either.

All of this coincided with our move to Nicaragua. Fortunately, I had more time to think and realized just how shocking it was. How could these doctors know that I had a condition considered Stage 1 Cancer and still have no recommendations? It was time to empower myself as a patient, do my own research, hire a wellness coach, and gain control over my immune system. I faced a truth that so many of us discover in our thirties: Health is in our hands, and we have to advocate for ourselves, because no one else will.

It turns out there was a lot I was doing wrong: the pill, tampons, panty liners, intimate soaps, wipes, synthetic underwear, eating sugar and processed foods, social drinking, stress.

———
[1] Loop Electrosurgical Excision Procedure

Thankfully, I also found out what I could start doing right away: exercising, eating real, quality foods, getting more sleep, relaxing, and developing a more spiritual life. My efforts paid off. Further testing showed that the HPV had not returned. I kept taking folic acid and closed that chapter, again.

My body worked well for three more years. I was living a different life, far away from the corporate world. Walking around town was a habit and also the easiest option, and I had become a regular yoga and HIIT practitioner thanks to my supportive and empowering friends in Granada. The fresh tropical fruits and vegetables in Nicaragua were not necessarily organic, and hopefully not GMO, but they were affordable. So was the vinegar I used to wash off the pesticides. I abstained from eating the obvious harmful foods, sticking to the Environmental Working Group's "Clean Fifteen," which was relatively easy even with the limited options at the two local supermarkets. I'd been on the pill for years. It was "convenient," though the numb limbs I experienced when first taking it should have alerted me to the fact that it wasn't as safe as everyone said it was. I decided to break up with the pill and make friends with condoms. With every change, it felt like my life was moving in the right direction.

Then, when I was thirty-two, my already short cycle became even shorter out of nowhere. I had always experienced twenty-one day cycles with heavy bleeding at the beginning. I got my period at age nine, when a visit to the endocrinologist confirmed that my body was about three years ahead of my actual age. The solution back then? Medroxyprogesterone to help balance out the estrogen. But now I was bleeding just two weeks after my last period. I'd never experienced a cycle this short. What was going on?

Dr. E, my gynecologist, did an ultrasound to determine if I had PCOS.[2] After finding nothing, she sent me home with a million-times-photocopied chart to track my cycle.

That didn't help. A few months later, I went to my trustworthy and dedicated endocrinologist, Dr. B, and after telling her the story, she couldn't believe my gyn had not ordered lab tests to check my hormones levels. I couldn't believe that either. Dr. B ordered new lab work, which showed that the abnormal bleeding was caused by low progesterone and high estrogen, a condition called estrogen dominance. She told me it was "easy to fix" with synthetic hormone pills, the same pills prescribed decades earlier by my doctor in Santo Domingo.

Thanks. But no thanks. That wasn't the solution for me.

It kept happening every other month—I thought maybe one ovary was having the problem. But after a year of suffering with this hormonal balance, I had to do something.

---

[2] Polycystic Ovarian Syndrome

I decided I would try the naturopathic way, with an integrative gynecologist who prescribed bioidentical hormones and advertised in Natural Awakenings, the free magazine at the entrance to Whole Foods. I knew this approach would take longer, and I didn't know if it would work, but somewhere inside me I felt it was the right choice and that I had time. I was not necessarily trying to get pregnant.

I went to pick up my medical records at Dr. E's office, my old gyn. The girl at the front desk knew I was about to change doctors. "Where are you going?" she whispered.

"I'm going to Dr. M.," I told her, "because she uses bioidentical hormones and I want to fix my hormones so I can start trying to have a baby."

"She won't be able to help you, even with bioidentical hormones. Go to this place," she said, handing me a business card from a center for fertility and genetics.

I thanked her, hugged her, and walked to my car in tears. As soon as I had the breath to speak, I called and asked for the earliest appointment with the doctor on the business card. That lead doctor didn't have any openings for weeks, but they offered me Dr. Karipcin, and I took her next open slot.

The Coral Gables fertility center was upscale and modern—white, silver, accented with orchids. Dr. K was beautiful and extremely sweet. She asked me about my background, marriage, career, blog, and health history, and then did an ultrasound before ordering dozens of additional tests. "Everything looks good," she said in her thick Turkish accent, rubbing the ultrasound wand over my pelvis with the help of cold gel. "Except that for your age, I don't see enough eggs."

That didn't worry me much at the moment. After all, she said things looked good. I went for the labs and came back to see her again. Claudio had labs done, too. His results showed low sperm morphology, which is a common condition among men in their thirties. Luckily for them, men renew their sperm every ninety days. Therefore, with lifestyle adjustments such as taking a multivitamin and reducing smoking and drinking, they can improve their fertility relatively quickly. My fertility picture was different. My anti-Mullerian hormone (AMH) was 0.03 (a normal reading for a woman ten years older than me) and my follicle-stimulating hormone (FSH) was 31 (panic high is 21). Dr. K's suspicions were right: I had diminished ovarian reserve. Ultra-low progesterone and high estrogen was another issue, just as the first lab results had showed. My adrenals were not functioning well either.

I broke into tears. All the reasons why I had delayed pregnancy started rushing through my head: uncertainty and lack of stability in my marriage, the cost of health insurance, working like crazy to save up enough money, stepping on a tack in Nicaragua, Zika (trying to conceive in the time of Zika sounds like the title of a Gabriel García Márquez novel). Sobbing, I wondered if I would ever be able to get pregnant.

Dr. K handed me a box of Kleenex. "I will hold your hand until you get pregnant," she said. It was as if she'd heard the question in my mind. She wrote on her small yellow pad, explaining the different options. First, two months of timed intercourse. If that didn't work, we should try IUI, and our last option was egg donors. IVF wouldn't be possible for me.

She asked the nurse to lead me to a private room where I could cry alone until I felt better. "You should be writing about this," she told me.

I went home devastated. Once again, I had to take charge of my health, my healing, and ultimately, my fertility. I knew every month was an opportunity and that I only needed one egg. I started Googling everything I could do to fight those lab results. I found invaluable tips and resources specific to my situation: probiotics, acupuncture, yoga, massage therapy, supplements, all kinds of foods, and seeding for fertility. A dear friend recommended health coach Beth Hill. I contacted her and we agreed to trade coaching practice hours as we were both finishing our programs. Beth took the time to go over my case, and gave me helpful advice ranging from nutrition tips to relaxation techniques. She inspired me to try new foods and helped me become more mindful about grocery shopping, meal planning, and time management. Her flexibility and understanding made our sessions possible, despite the challenges of my ever-changing schedule. Our work continued during a five-country tour with a rock band in South America when I was sleep deprived, out of my routine, and attempting to adapt my fertility diet to what I could find at Latin American markets and restaurants. I always carried a suitcase full of food staples and supplements.

Then the most amazing thing happened. Four months after we started our program, with the aid of timed intercourse, faith, and divine mercy, I was able to conceive naturally. As my prenatal yoga teacher would say: "My baby and I are happy, healthy, and wholly." I even got the bonus of an extremely "fast and easy" childbirth. Thank God.

With the thorough diagnosis of Dr. K, the guidance of my health and wellness coach Beth, and a positive mindset, I embarked on a mindful journey to health—and received the gift of a lifetime. As a message of hope, please know that no matter where you are in your health or fertility journey, anything is possible. My baby and I are living proof.

Abnormal Pap smears, decreased fertility, and hormonal imbalances are just some of the pressing sexual health issues that we can encounter in our thirties. They are worthy of close attention, because they impact not only our health but our relationships with ourselves and our partners. In order to explore this topic further, I interviewed Dr. Sonjia Kenya, best-selling author of *Sex in South Beach*, certified sexologist, and associate professor of medicine at the University of Miami Miller School of Medicine.

What are the biggest changes we experience in our thirties?

In your thirties, you are finally ready—to have adventures, to try out relationships with people of different races or religions, to shed your good girl image. Earlier in your sexual experiences, you were concerned about how your behavior was interpreted and what your partner might think: "What if I ask for this or that? Condom or no condom? Toy or no toy?" Now you are more confident and liberated.

For women, libido heightens in their thirties and their desire peaks. Meanwhile, a man's desire declines during this time. Many men begin experiencing erectile dysfunction in their late thirties and hence we have the "cougar movement." It's nothing new; it's just that a man in his twenties has a libido that generally matches that of a woman in her thirties. Otherwise, everything is particular with women and with human sexuality.

As far as science goes, everyone is different, and everyone has a different sex drive, a different amount of testosterone. For women, a lot of our sex drive is tied into how happy we are with our bodies, how much stress we experience, and how relaxed we are. Women can only enjoy optimal sexual relationships when they're relaxed. Women who are stressed out have a hard time enjoying sex.

During your thirties, you want to find someone who has a libido that matches yours, someone who's in tune with you sexually. If you don't like having sex, maybe you're fine with it once a month or once in a while. But if your partner wants sex every day, that's not a good match. The best advice that my mother ever gave me was, "Wait until your thirties to get married," because you change more between your twenties and thirties than in any other time in your whole life. Get to know yourself better. That will help you find the right partner.

Levels of sexual experience matter, too. I work with a couple that has been together since the woman was eighteen. The man is her only sex partner ever, but he has had numerous partners. Sex has become boring and routine. They don't even have it anymore. They're stuck with what they did when she was eighteen and that's what they are still doing twenty years later. You can get stuck at this age, or you can start thinking of sex as a continuum, a way to grow up and try things together.

Almost all women equate sex with love, no matter what they say. Some women think they will have sex with no strings attached, but they call me three to four weeks later, saying, "I thought I could do it." But they can't, because they're wondering, "Is he sleeping with other people? Is he just using me?" I try to remind women that a lot of the time, we volunteer for these situations. I do think it's much more important in your thirties to establish boundaries before you have sex or establish the terms and context of the relationship. A lot of women get their feelings hurt in their thirties.

What are your top recommendations for having healthy sex in your thirties?

Don't do things or get yourself into situations that make you uncomfortable. Ever. Because you will always regret it. It's like that guy you settle for—we've all had that guy who is just not what we are looking for but we settle for him anyway. And guess what? He still ends up breaking your heart. If you do get yourself into an uncomfortable or unpleasant situation, you might put up mental barriers: "All men are like this," or "All people are like this." I work with women in their thirties and forties who have had traumatic sexual experiences, and in some cases they put themselves in those situations. They were intoxicated, or they were with someone who did not respect their boundaries, and as a result they cannot enjoy sex anymore. It's terrible. Avoid situations that might result in negative experiences. Period.

Another thing: Know yourself, know your smell, know your discharge. Because with the most common STDs—chlamydia and gonorrhea—50 percent of women have no symptoms. And if you have gonorrhea that goes untreated, you are going to end up infertile. You have to get everything treated. If you ever have a question, go to the doctor. There is no sense in driving yourself crazy worrying about it, just go. Be sure to get your annual check-ups, because everyone is going to have HPV (we've all been exposed to it). It's the most common thing, and it can turn into cervical cancer. Women are more likely to experience health issues in their thirties, and because we are the receivers in sex, we're at a greater risk.

People forget that in our thirties we are just as likely to contract a sexually transmitted disease. I talk to a lot of people in their thirties who are professionally successful but not practicing safe sex behavior. It's almost like they're teenagers again. They think because they know this person and they're a friend of a friend and they have a good job that somehow it's okay. They take silly risks. They forget that HIV and herpes are still prevalent.

Communicate with your partner about their physical and emotional health, but particularly their physical health. You should be able to go to the clinic together, and do all of your tests together. You should be able to communicate about these things. If you can't even talk, if it makes you giggle, or laugh, or feel embarrassed, how do you think you're going to share your body with this person? If you're too embarrassed to talk about it, then you should not be risking your life. In my book, *Sex in South Beach*, I wrote that if someone can't answer "Who? What? When? Where? Why?" (Who is your doctor? What did you see them for? When did you go? Where do they practice? And why did you seek medical help?), then that person is high-risk. At the end of the day, you want to feel free when you are having sex, which means you must have the ability to communicate.

Everyone should experiment and learn, especially people in committed relationships. You might think that because you know everything about your husband and are planning to be with him forever that your sex life is going to get boring. Don't let it.

Continue experimenting and learning. I'm a big fan of role-playing because studies have shown that female sex drive decreases the longer we are with someone. Whereas men will pretty much have sex with whoever is lying next to them. For women, you might not feel like having sex yourself, but once you put on a costume or you have an alter ego, then you're not even you. You are acting and it is more fun because now you are this hot chick that your husband just met, and your husband is that cute massage therapist. I encourage people to walk into adult/sex stores and look around and learn. By experimenting and learning, you keep it fresh and fun—because sex is supposed to be fun.

Society has conditioned us to think that people are just supposed to know how to have great sex, which is a myth. We get no education on it. You learn how to drive before you drive—and we need to learn the basics of how the body works since it's born with its own sex drive. In a perfect world, everyone would know how to protect themselves from STDs, they would know how often to go to the doctor's office for check-ups, and they would know about pleasure. Because that is what this conversation is about. We all know how to have sex to procreate, to have children, but do we know enough about sex to make it a pleasurable part of our lives as we age? Our bodies will change, we will get more wrinkles, and we will not always want to have intercourse. Women will go through menopause, men will go through erectile dysfunction, but how do we keep that intimate bond alive? Having conversations about sex and sexual desire is important: just because he can't get an erection doesn't mean that he doesn't want to be touched, and vice versa.

How does all of this affect relationship dynamics in our thirties?

In your thirties, you start to experience a new pressure that you didn't have in your twenties: "Am I going to get married? Am I going to have kids? How much time do I have?" When you're younger, you don't care how much money a partner has or where their family comes from or what class they're in, but all of a sudden in your thirties you realize, "Oh no, he is Muslim and I'm Jewish," or "He doesn't have a job—how's he going to make money?" That cute bartender that you would've dated in your twenties is no longer a real possibility. You start thinking, "I don't want someone with mental problems. I don't want someone who can't get a job, or who likes me too much and suddenly they're stalking me." We are more concerned with how appropriate our partner is—are they going to fit in with our friends and family?

A lot of people in their thirties are divorced, or they have children. That is something we need to consider when we get into sexual relationships. I always knew that I didn't want someone with children because I need to be the first priority in a relationship and someone who has kids needs to make their children their first priority. I got married rather late. I remember my mother telling me, "You're going to have to give that one up. You're going to have to start dating people with kids," and I was resistant to doing that. Fortunately, my husband did not have any children.

Body image is another common concern. The first time we normally experience body image issues is in our thirties. When you are eighteen you just look great. You don't have any wrinkles, and your body is tight. But now you're asking, "How do I look in this? Do I look fat? Does he think I look fat?" His body image concerns also come up. Guys tend to stay fit for a long time, and then they start to get potbellies. And if you're getting together in your thirties, he probably knows you've had other experiences: he is worried about how he measures up to your former partners. All of this now starts to enter into relationships.

Men and women are more health-conscious as they get older. When I was thirty, I was in the Cayman Islands, partying, working two days a week at a medical school, writing a sex column, having cocktails at ten in the morning. Now my husband and I take our probiotics every day. We are old enough to know we need things to stay healthy, and we are old enough to afford it. I had a genetics test done by my doctor because of my age, and he told my husband, "She has the genetics of a twenty-year-old. You don't have to trade her in for a younger model—you can have as many kids as you want." He talked about how some young people come in with all kinds of health issues, and what's most important is not necessarily the age of the woman but the choices she makes. Science has shown that fertility does decrease in our thirties, but I think these statistics are exaggerated because they are only collected at infertility treatment centers. A woman like me who gave birth at thirty-nine years old, who got pregnant without trying at thirty-eight, a girlfriend who just gave birth at forty-two, and another girlfriend who is thirty-seven—none of us is included in those statistics, because we didn't go to a doctor to get help. The real question is: Are you healthy? There are cases of preeclampsia in teenagers and women in their twenties because they are unhealthy. But if you are thirty-nine, healthy, and fit, you are going to have a beautiful pregnancy and everything will be just fine.

Healthy people want to have better sex lives. They're more likely to enjoy sex and more likely to choose a partner who is going to communicate with them, someone they'll be able to grow with. Partners keep each other healthy. Your husband is not going to die of cancer because you're not going to let him. He's going to get his physical every year because you are going to make him do it, and vice versa. He is going to make sure you're going to all of your doctor's appointments when you get pregnant. You are partners in this. And science has shown that people with a satisfying sex life enjoy better health, are more successful, and earn more money. Other than drinking water, eating, and sleeping, sex is arguably the most important aspect of our health and long-term happiness. If you're not doing it, it affects you. And if you're doing it, it affects you. It affects everyone. Now, a healthy sex life doesn't necessarily mean that you are having sex on a regular basis; it could be that I am communicating effectively with my partner and he is giving me an intimate massage. It just means you and your partner are both satisfied in your intimate relationship.

And the same goes for success: If you have a partner who supports you, then you're going to be more successful at your job. When you are happy and successful, you are much more likely to enjoy sex; it all ties in together. When you have money, you can enjoy a romantic weekend or dinner, all those little things.

Do you think spirituality plays a role in how our relationships grow over time?

I've dealt with couples where one partner thinks that having sex for reasons other than procreation is a sin and the other partner wants to have sex for fun. This is a problem. I do think it is important to find someone who is on your same spiritual path and shares the same beliefs regarding sex. Do you think that God wants you to enjoy your sex life or not? My perspective is that sex is a form of pleasure. God has given us this amazing body and he does want us to have pleasurable experiences—and sex can be pleasurable. It can be a way to celebrate your body, but not everyone believes that. So I should not be with someone who thinks that you only have sex for procreation or that you should only have sex missionary-style or that sex always involves intercourse and no foreplay.

This is especially important if you go through the process of childbirth. I'm now breastfeeding my baby and some of my girlfriends have not been successful in breast-feeding, and I believe that a lot of it is due to lack of support from their husbands. One of my girlfriend's husband is really critical of her body. But another man might find that beautiful, how you can feed your baby naturally—this is a miraculous experience. My husband still finds me sexy and I walk around the house pumping half the time.

DR. SONJIA is the best-selling author of *Sex in South Beach*, a certified sexologist, and an associate professor of medicine at the University of Miami Miller School of Medicine. She received her bachelor's degree from UCLA and earned two master's degrees along with her doctorate at Columbia University in New York (also where Dr. Ruth trained!). During grad school and a post-doctoral fellowship for the National Institutes of Health, Dr. Sonjia conducted research on sex problems, sexually transmitted diseases, and sexual functioning.

Another unavoidable truth in our thirties is how our metabolism slows down, bringing physical changes, new weight management challenges, and overall health issues for both women and men. I would like to end this section with an interview with Angelique Millis Huntsman, an Austin-based certified fitness professional, journalist, and lifestyle coach, who was generous enough to share her transformative story and healthy lifestyle expertise.

What inspired you to become a certified fitness professional and lifestyle coach?

My interest in health and fitness began in college when I was trying to reverse some bad lifestyle habits that I had developed. Just like all students, I knew exactly how to study under pressure, party like a rock star, and "burn the candle at both ends," juggling schoolwork, extracurricular activities, and my social life. I was a huge emotional eater; I would eat when I was stressed, happy, or sad. Before I knew it, all those late nights at Denny's and trips to the McDonald's drive-thru had added up and I found myself forty pounds heavier. I had also started smoking cigarettes and drinking beer with friends almost every night. Fitness was the farthest thing from my mind.

My "aha" moment was when I was walking with a couple of girlfriends and caught a glimpse of our reflections in a store window. I noticed that they were so much thinner than me. When we would go shopping, I was ashamed to come out of the fitting room and I was embarrassed because I would secretly have to ask the sales lady to bring me a bigger size. I felt drained from the life I was leading and I knew that if I didn't make a change soon, my weight would continue to balloon and my health would suffer.

When I first began my transformation, I immersed myself in fitness magazines, books, and websites, seeking answers. There is a world of knowledge at our fingertips, so I took it upon myself to become educated. I also had a vision of what I wanted to look and feel like and I was going to stop at nothing to attain it. I endured many struggles and obstacles in embracing a new lifestyle, and later even more obstacles maintaining it. Through my own trial and error, I have concluded that there is no magic pill or potion for getting fit. It is not something that can be learned from simply reading a book—it is about applying the knowledge in a way that works for you.

Because society has made it so acceptable to take the easy way out and "drive-thru" your cares away at the end of a stressful workday, it took a lot of self-empowerment and discipline for me to break free from that mentality. I had to learn how to kick bad habits by staring them square in the face and understanding that there were no shortcuts. In the end, it came down to desire, patience, and applied knowledge. In total, I lost forty pounds and five dress sizes, but let me make clear that it did not happen overnight.

Fitness is a lifestyle, not just a "look." I think it's fantastic that people get motivated to achieve that look but they have to be realistic by setting small, detailed goals. It takes time to build muscle, time to perfect your diet habits, and even more time to balance your new habits and transform your life through fitness. There needs to be a balance of patience and persistence—you may not get the results you want right away, but if you are focused on your goals, it will happen. You need to enjoy the process and love yourself enough to do things the right way. I say this because it took me a few years to finally piece it all together. The new disciplines and habits I learned through this experience have allowed me to evolve in other areas of my life and have also given me a new purpose and sense of self. I challenged myself to compete in some bikini/fitness shows and a year later, I changed careers and started my own fitness business where I began to help others shape their bodies and transform their lives.

What particular health needs arise in our thirties?

When I turned thirty a couple years ago, despite all of the exercise that I had been doing over the years to maintain my transformation, it became inevitable that my body was slowly changing. Although I had maintained my weight loss and healthy lifestyle for a couple years, my body was not as forgiving for any back-to-back "cheat" days that I used to be able to get away with.

Your thirties will reveal any bad habits you formed in your twenties. If you basked in the sun for too long, your skin may begin to show signs of premature aging. It is important to use products infused with antioxidants (like CoQ10 or vitamins A, C, and E) to repair damage done by sun, pollution, stress, and the natural process of aging. Your hormones also begin to change and it may become more difficult to exercise due to stress, work and family responsibilities, and other time constraints. The good news is that even if you have not exercised a day in your life, it is never too late to embrace a healthy lifestyle! The key is to form healthy habits that will help you age with more grace.

Because your bone density changes in your thirties, it is of the utmost importance to make weight training a priority to decrease the risk of osteoporosis. It will also strengthen your abdominal core, support your joints, and help you maintain a natural, aligned posture. Plus, weight training will boost your metabolism and help shape your body, so it's a win-win situation and one of the best habits anyone can form.

What is the impact of nutrition and fitness on our energy levels and the aging process?

People spend millions of dollars a year on quick fixes and plastic surgery to look younger, when at the end of the day the answer lies in food. "Let thy food be thy medicine..." It all goes back to Hippocrates. Fitness and nutrition are the fountain of youth! Eating a diet rich in calcium, vitamin D, magnesium, and folic acid will help support your body's needs and make you feel full, energetic, and healthy. Defy the aging process without pills or cosmetic procedures by juicing every morning, eating leafy greens, and consuming a balanced, whole food diet. Also, avoiding sugar and caffeine will help improve your skin's elasticity. Eating protein will strengthen your hair, skin, and nails, and your energy levels will skyrocket when you begin to exercise diligently. The bottom line is that preserving your youth is a choice. At the end of a long day of work, you can choose to go home and have a glass of wine or you can choose to go to "happy hour" at the gym—I say choose the barbells over the bar! The end result will outweigh any sugary cocktail and you will improve your energy, release endorphins, and go home feeling great!

What is the relationship between physical health and mental health?

I am a firm believer that a strong mind creates a strong body. Strengthening your mind and your spirit will also give you the tools to cope with life's stressors in a more positive, productive, and healthy way. If you are in a negative mental state, by default, your physical health will suffer. Caring for your health and your body is a decision, and if you are not in the right place to prioritize it, it is likely to be overlooked or neglected. Every thought you think and every word you say is an affirmation, whether it is negative, neutral, or positive. The mind is truly a powerful thing and experts believe that even the most negative mindset can be reprogrammed through positive affirmations. This practice has been proven to replace dysfunctional beliefs with newly adopted positive beliefs. Choose a mantra or affirmation that you say out loud at least once a day. Some experts have proven that even writing down the affirmation ten to twenty times per day will help imprint it in your mind. Here are some examples of mantras and positive affirmations:

Affirmations for a Strong Mind, Body, and Spirit
- I am organized
- I am intelligent
- I will get out of my own way
- I will be fueled by my passion to succeed
- I will be led by my dreams
- I am strong and beautiful
- I am in control of my thoughts
- I make healthy choices
- I choose to nourish my body with healthy food
- I choose to exercise regularly
- My body heals quickly and easily
- Every cell in my body vibrates with energy

Are there any links between our health and our relationships, spirituality, career, finances, and lifestyle in general?

Absolutely! When you feel good and are getting adequate nutrition, exercise, water, and sleep, you are more likely to focus and succeed in all areas of your life. A healthy lifestyle will make your energy flourish and along with the desire to improve any specific area in your life, you will have the focus to do it! Whether you want better communication skills in your relationships, improved decision making abilities in your finances and career, or overall life balance, it all stems from a healthy mental, physical, and emotional state.

What are your insights about healthy body image and disorders such as anorexia, bulimia, obesity, starvation, pre-obesity, food addiction, and overtraining?

For years, mass media's influence and what it portrays as "beautiful" has left women with body image issues as they compare what they see in the mirror to the overly filtered and photoshopped ads in glossy magazines. When we don't have a healthy body image, we often fall victim to eating disorders such as binging and purging, or even overtraining at the gym. It is very easy to resort to obsessive calorie counting, ephedrine pill-popping, and excessive exercising if you do not establish a healthy body image from the start. My best advice to anyone out there who is on the brink of their fitness journey is to be realistic with your expectations. It is best not to compare yourself to others or let the number on the scale define you. Just work on making the best decisions possible—eating right, sleeping well, and striving to attain the healthiest version of you.

—— **ANGELIQUE MILLIS HUNTSMAN** is a certified fitness professional, journalist, and lifesyle coach living in Austin, TX. A weight loss success story who combated her vices and transformed her physique by losing nearly forty pounds and five dress sizes, Angelique has transcended her passion for health and fitness into motivating and educating others to reach their fitness potential. Angelique is firmly dedicated to helping others improve their lives, and because leading a fit lifestyle often involves a degree of sacrifice and discipline that many struggle with, she writes empowering content geared towards "fitness beginners" that both inspires and guides readers as they embark or re-embark on their fitness journey.

Spirit

One night during my late twenties, I was sleeping when I heard a voice call my name, vivid and close. I sat up in bed. My husband was asleep beside me. I reached for my phone and found Juan Luis Guerra's Christian song to use as a prayer: "I don't need pills to sleep if you are with me, all my dreams blossom when you whisper in my ears…" I repeated those words until I fell back asleep. That was the first time I heard the voice of God.

Approaching thirty, I realized that the only area of my life with no goals was my spirituality. As a girl I had felt religion everywhere. I remember my mother tucking me into bed and saying her favorite prayer: *"Con Dios me acuesto, con Dios me levanto, la Virgen María y el Espíritu Santo."* Religion was in her expressions; it was in our voice of conscience as a family, and in our hopes. We would speak openly to the saints, sometimes jokingly: *"San Isidro Labrador, quita la lluvia y pon el sol."* San Antonio was the saint who helped me find lost items—including boyfriends! We often visited my maternal grandmother in her hometown, Higüey, and we would bring bright red flowers of offering to the country's patroness, *La Virgen de la Altagracia*. My paternal grandmother was more adventurous when it came to religion. She experimented with different versions of Christianity, and we were all okay with that, as long as she didn't hurt herself from all the kneeling.

As a college student at a scientific university where religion was de-emphasized (I remember one of my teachers saying that Jesus and his twelve apostles were the first political party), I was given an assignment for my sociology course: to visit every church in the Dominican Republic— Mormons, Baptists, Adventists, Evangelicals, Catholics, and Jehovah's Witnesses. The Church of Jesus Christ of Latter-day Saints temple was the most technologically advanced and luxurious place I had ever been. Mormons were well known in the DR for being young American gentlemen, walking or biking around the city with their crisp white shirts and black pants. Some people claimed they were spies. Other "churches" were informal spaces in garages or houses that had been adapted as places of worship, often with loud services (*"¡Arrepiéntanse! ¡Cristo viene!"*). The Seventh-day Adventist Church sold its own line of natural products. I didn't need to go far to find the Jehovah's Witnesses—they visit houses door by door, promoting their faith and giving away their magazines, *Watchtower* and *Awake!* (*El Atalaya* and *Despertad!* in Spanish). After all that research I remained Catholic. It was familiar to me and a big part of our country's culture. Yet the assignment did make me think about how broadly defined religion can be.

Religion was an important entry on my "Before-I-Get-Married-To-Do-List," but I just didn't have the time. Through my friend Kris, Claudio and I found a multilingual Catholic priest for our beach wedding, and I vowed to make room for religion in my life, to search and question and define my faith. I knew God was "there" for me; I just had no idea how to get "there."

Exactly two weeks before I turned thirty, I went on an Emmaus Women's Retreat, a program open to people of all Christian faiths. My friend Saskya had invited me and encouraged me to go multiple times before. I figured if I had regular check-ups with my gynecologist and took my car to the mechanic for a tune-up, I should also set aside at least a weekend for this spiritual "boot camp." Claudio and my younger sister Carla dropped me off at the parking lot of a random church in Hialeah, FL. After a brief introduction where we enjoyed Cuban *pastelitos* and *croquetas*, we were asked to give up our cell phones for the next three days. I got on a bus full of strangers that took us to a remote location. I started crying the minute I sat down.

I didn't know anybody there—and nobody knew me. I felt anonymous, invisible, but also acknowledged and understood. Even forgiven and loved. I remember being at the back of the chapel, trying to decide whether I wanted to stand in front. I was hesitant, still figuring out my feelings about the whole retreat, and that level of visibility felt like a very public commitment. When I finally made my way up to the front, I saw the image of Jesus that looked cold and serious from afar was actually smiling. "Come to Me" the picture said.

Most of the women were around my age. Everybody looked mature. It was obvious they were making a sacrifice to take time away and go deeper into their own lives. I didn't know anything about their pasts and we didn't get to share details. But I could imagine their stories based on their emotional reactions to others' testimonials. Some of them would cry silently. Other would explode weeping.

I found company, encouragement, guidance, inspiration, and hope among those women (there were even some hardcore *Fifty Shades of Grey* fans in the mix). One of the exercises used a phrase that struck me as important, and still does: "God's time is not human time." By the end of the weekend, I had a heart full of love plus a bag full of gifts and letters from old and new friends, and still, my baggage felt much lighter. Reading those letters seven years later still brings me to tears.

The retreat organizers secretly contacted Claudio, encouraging him to ask my friends and family to write letters showing their love and support for this new spiritual journey. He recruited Carla as an accomplice for that mission and the results were heart-melting. Some letters were one paragraph, some were three pages. My little nephews, Ian and

Zahir, filled their letters with photos and drawings. I laughed and cried as I read them. All of them were filled with love, wisdom, and hope. Others contained big news like baby announcements. Most of them took me through memories from my childhood, teenage years, and twenties. "When you take one step towards God," said one letter, "he takes ten steps towards you." My late friend Leana wrote that one.

I'm still getting to know my God, and learning to accept his will. Though I'm convinced of the benefits of spirituality, I disagree with some religious institutions, their history, culture, and actions. For now, I'm concentrating on developing a close, conscious relationship with God. I talk to God and read the Bible because it brings me peace. But so does reading quotes from the Buddha and copies of *Watchtower* and *Awake!,* which my Nicaraguan seamstress always gives me, practicing yoga, enjoying a good nap or a full night of sleep, and helping someone in need. I have come to see everything in my life as a spiritual practice, an ongoing attempt to understand and find fulfillment. And in Nicaragua, I'm reminded of how strongly religion can influence culture—the pre-dawn *bombas* and processions for *La Purísima* every December 8th (Claudio and I lie in bed listening to the 4 a.m. trumpets), the inviting sounds of the Catholic church bells, the courageous amateurs singing sidewalk hymns, the recordings of the rosary played at chapels every afternoon.

I ask God to put wisdom in my heart and wise words in my mouth. I want to be more compassionate. I want to act with more grace. For me, it all started with the Bible. But it could just as easily have been the Koran, the Vedas, Tripitaka, or any other holy book. I encourage you to find what speaks to you, and to be open to exploring spirituality, self-love, inner peace, faith, acceptance, and gratitude—in you and everyone around you.

I met Warren Ogden during my first month in Granada at Pure, the natural health and fitness center he founded in 2006. He noticed that I attended yoga classes every morning and mentioned the theory that we need to do something for twenty-one days in order for it to become a habit. At that point I didn't know if making yoga a habit was my goal, but I told him I'd also heard that it takes four weeks for us to notice a change in our own bodies, eight weeks for our partners to notice, and twelve weeks for everybody else to notice. I kept visiting Pure, reading the books in their library, exploring different classes and workshops, and that was the beginning of my yoga practice and of brief, meaningful conversations with Warren and other teachers who supported my spiritual growth. Below are some notes from one of our enriching talks:

How do you define spiritual practice?

A spiritual practice is one where an individual proactively seeks and puts in the effort to develop their own happiness, internal peace, calm, and feeling of interconnectivity. It's an entirely internal experience, like a laboratory where we investigate what works for us and what doesn't.

What advice would you give to someone who wants to start a spiritual practice?

Develop your ability to observe what's happening in the moment. It requires a lot of effort, but as you increase your awareness, you will shift how you interact with the world. Every little bit of effort you put into it, you get back.

So many things that arise in our lives initially strike us as disappointments, aggravations, or frustrations—because we have expectations of the way they are supposed to be. "I should be successful at this," "I shouldn't feel disappointed or upset." But we can learn to let go of expectations and feel what we're actually feeling in any given moment. That, for me, is the beginning of a spiritual practice.

What are some of the obstacles to spirituality?

It's part of our culture to always seek the new. The key is to do something that makes you feel more present in the moment. More calm. More alive.

We have two different levels in our thinking mind. There's a layer that is connected to ideas—it's bouncing thoughts and answering questions. And then we have a lower layer of more fundamental beliefs, of truths that we feel are essential. When we observe our thoughts, we can ask: "What serves me? Is that feeling me? Is it going to help me create internal peace and calm? Is it going to make my life more enjoyable?"

—— **WARREN OGDEN** founded Pure in 2006 with the mission "to promote and engender the physical, spiritual and emotional well-being of its clients, team members and the larger community of Granada, Nicaragua." Warren began studying both fitness and yoga twenty years ago at Duke University. He has been personal training and teaching yoga for the last thirteen years. Warren studied yoga in Rishikesh and Dharamshala, India, and completed his 200-hour yoga teacher training program with the Holistic Yoga School and his 500-hour advanced studies with the Kashmir Shaivism School of Yoga in India. Warren is also an AcroYoga instructor, having completed AcroYoga Montreal's teacher training in 2019.

— *Work* —

I almost quit my second career before I launched it. After more than fifteen years in live events and television production management, I needed a new challenge, a new direction, so I enrolled in a professional life coaching certification program at the University of Miami. I had seen an ad on Facebook and liked the curriculum. Then I asked for a discount, got it, and registered while Claudio wondered whether it was the right time for me to go back to school.

The first module was called "Deep Hearing." Hearing, I thought: interesting. In my mind coaching was going to be more about talking. And I was ready to talk! Growing up, I had wanted to be center stage: on-air, talent, a ballerina or any kind of non-starving artist, a fashion or home designer, a teacher, an advertising pro—I went through everything. The most exciting part of ballet school was always performing at the annual show. Later on I went to castings for commercials, trained for the news, volunteered for a college radio show, got professional pictures, taped amateur video demos, took workshops, and followed on and off the directions to showbiz success. I thought coaching would be similar. I would shower people with strategies and tips. My breakthrough wisdom would inspire coachees to change their lives. I pictured myself on a stage in front of hundreds of people, wearing the same white suit that I bought for the presentation of my master's thesis and then used years later for my thirtieth birthday photo shoot. That's the kind of coach I was going to be.

Then I learned the truth about coaching: it's not about me. Kind of a surprise at first, but it started to sink in with each new lesson. It turns out that coaching is always about the client, and the client is the expert. I ask powerful questions and listen to the answers. It's not my job to solve problems or offer opinions. It's my job to "meet" clients where they are, to hold space for them as they gain the awareness necessary to shift their perspectives and take action toward self-defined solutions.

Listening is harder than I thought. I saw myself as a good listener—another role I could naturally play. But listening means stopping multitasking, immersing myself in the conversation, being quiet, and being present. It means not interrupting (that's a hard one), not judging (also difficult), and not always referring to my own experience—we're all unique.

One solution doesn't fit all. Silence can be a useful part of a conversation. The simple truth is that just being heard, just having someone bear witness to your thoughts and feelings, can make a big difference.

With coaching, I've made an important professional shift. I now have the opportunity to *give* attention, support, accountability, and encouragement, instead of my past focus on *getting* credits, contacts, and status. The most fulfilling moments for me are when I get to share my experience with those who are just starting their careers, at whatever age. I especially love interviewing interns and recent grads, training them and working alongside them, and of course celebrating their success. I admit I've made a few interns cry by telling them to fight for what they really want instead of settling for an office job connected to what they really want. I try never to sugarcoat the facts.

I am not afraid of being displaced by the new generation. Today, I thank that highly paid TV executive who said he would hire "the next twenty-two year old" if I was not okay with not getting a raise. He saw me as an obstacle instead of someone worth investing in. I'm the complete opposite: I embrace the curiosity and energy of the newcomers, and whenever they ask me for advice, I gladly offer my perspective.

Any working mom will tell you that your career takes on all kinds of new challenges once you're balancing it with raising a child. So far I've done a few major coaching projects as a new mom, including two vision board workshops at the Artsy Hive, a pottery painting studio close to my house and even closer to my heart. I brought my baby to meetings there, and to the Condé Nast LatAm offices and Brockway Library when I went to pick up magazines. My oldest sister held him while I was getting my hair and nails done by the local Nica ladies, and then daddy took care of him during the events, where I had the privilege of coaching former classmates and colleagues.

My days in entertainment aren't completely over (when work calls, I answer)—but they are different. I pushed four-month-old Luca in a stroller to a recruiting event for my first production gig as a working mom. My sister Carla took care of him during the show (and took a day off from her own job to do it). I left breast milk, three different brands of milk formula, multiple bottles and nipples, clothes, diapers, wipes, toys, and instructions, including local police contact info. As I drove to the venue, I was surprised to feel so at peace leaving my child for the first time. I knew he was in great hands.

I arrived a few minutes late (working on that, can't even blame the kid) and started rolling. Only a couple hours had passed when I got a text from Carla. She asked me to come back home and pick them up because Luca didn't want to take the bottle. I told the closest members of the production team that I had to step out, drove an hour to get home, fed Luca, and then drove them back with me for another hour (luckily Miami's lovely traffic had not officially started, but the event was on the opposite side of the city).

That was only the beginning of three long days of work with my child onsite. Carla stayed in a dressing room with no windows or electronics for two, ten-hour days, babysitting her nephew so I could make some money. My husband came on the third day and did the same.

So many things still strike me about that experience: For brief moments, I felt like an actress, breastfeeding during breaks with my family entourage on set. I felt grateful to have the support and flexibility of my blood and work families. I felt sad and frustrated for the millions of women who don't have access to childcare (or elderly care), which limits their financial freedom and keeps them out of the workforce and even society. "It takes a village to raise a child." Yes, it does. It takes a family, a community, and a village.

These days, my most important titles are Mom, Wife, Daughter, Sister, Cousin, Friend, Coach, Speaker, Producer of My Dreams, and EIC of Personal & Family Affairs. I haven't totally lost those early dreams of production and fame, but I now know the price of those prized opportunities, and also the joy of giving back. I wouldn't mind trading my ambition and ultimate career aspirations for peace of mind, family time, and quality of life. I'm still proud of my resume, but I'm prouder of the lessons I've learned along the way.

Of course, I haven't figured everything out. The constant challenge I face now is re-designing my career and business ventures to suit my ideal lifestyle, to align my work with my needs and values as a professional and as a person. Does this sound familiar? Ideas are always welcome! And I'm always on the hunt for balance. That's why I talked with Cindy Goodman, a veteran journalist, blogger, and social media strategist, while she was in a taxi in New York. Goodman is a working mother of three on a quest to keep up with health, wellness, and lifestyle trends without sacrificing work-life balance.

What inspired you to write about work-life balance?

My own struggle as a journalist trying to meet deadlines, and balancing that with raising three children when my husband worked long hours. It was all part of my personal experience. I had just had my third child when I suggested that I should start writing on this topic, because I saw there was a big need for it.

I was doing fine before I had kids. I was working long hours, I was married and it was okay. I was balancing, but once I started having kids, I realized how difficult it was to balance family and work. The expectations were not even as great at that time because we had less technology. Now it's even harder—companies are expecting you to work longer and answer email and phone calls at all hours. It's much harder for young women today because of all the technology and all the expectations.

What is the ideal relationship between work and our relationships, health, spirituality, finances, and lifestyle?

It all depends on what you get fulfillment from—that's something that I have learned over the years writing about balance. Some people are very fulfilled by work; some are more fulfilled by their personal life. It's about what fulfills you and how much time you want to spend doing that.

Why are so many women burning out in their thirties?

People are trying to do so much so soon. A lot of women in their thirties are running businesses, and that is extremely time consuming. For a lot of women in their thirties, that's when you are struggling the most to be successful in your career. During that time it's easy to burn out. That's when you have to pay attention and ask yourself: Am I spending the right time doing the right things? The things that make me the happiest?

Should we consider making choices and sacrifices between career and family?

Sometimes you have to sacrifice. When you are in your thirties, mostly in your early thirties, you have to sacrifice. Sometimes it's just dating, relationships, spending time with your husband, or whatever you prefer, you have to make hard choices. Ask yourself: Am I going to put in the extra hours to arrive where I need to be? Single people struggle as much as people with families trying to find balance between work and their outside lives.

How is the work-life balance situation in the rest of the world?

A lot of my columns got picked up by newspapers in other countries, such as India. Work-life balance happens to be an issue around the world; I see the global interest. Some countries have better benefits for working families. Here in the States, the family-friendly policies and benefits that we offer are not as good as in other countries, but in general the issue of balancing work and family is a concern as more women are in the workplace.

What small changes could help us achieve career advancement and a balanced life-style?

It helps to have a role model, to look at somebody who is successful in the career that you are in and seems to have balance. Think: What is that person doing right that maybe I can model myself after? A lot of us see people and say, "I don't want to be like them." Look for who you would like to be, what opportunities they are taking advantage of, and follow their lead.

How can we demand and promote better work-life balance policies at our companies?

Speak out. Sometimes women are so afraid to speak out, ask questions, and offer suggestions. We are so afraid that if we show any signs of difficulty balancing, it's going to cost us in our career. In my own situation, I asked for flexibility, and I showed them what they were going to get in return. They knew I was a good worker, that I was going to put in 110 percent. Therefore, when I asked for a four-day workweek, they gave it to me. I wouldn't have known it was possible if I hadn't asked. We have to show our employer that it will work for them, that if they change their policies and show flexibility, they are going to keep these women, and they are going to keep working parents. Men should speak up, too, for their wives and their mothers.

Can we have it all: health, family, leisure, spiritual development, personal fulfillment, and career advancement?

It's possible. You might have to re-evaluate your dreams. You might have to trade being a top surgeon at a top hospital and having five kids for being a good surgeon at a good hospital and having two kids. It's possible to have fulfilling work and a fulfilling life, within reason.

—— **CINDY GOODMAN** is a working mother, award-winning journalist, blogger, content provider, social media strategist, digital copywriter, and former business reporter with a nationally-distributed newspaper column that offered insightful tips and trends on work-life balance for more than a decade.

- Money -

When I was four years old, I asked my mom why she had money and I didn't. "Because I work," she said, and in that moment I decided I would grow up as quickly as possible, to work, make money, and buy everything I wanted—like new clothes, jewelry, a bike, and those giant swirl lollipops you could buy at El Conde, a pedestrian street close to Santo Domingo's Zona Colonial.

I learned to balance schoolwork with what I considered "real work." I read all my academic books the summer before I entered second grade so I could concentrate on learning the multiplication tables, designing dresses and houses, and, of course, making money. At lunchtime, I would devour my cookies and homemade lemonade while my affluent classmates were exchanging coveted Garfield letter sheets that are now vintage stationery. I'd wait until they finished their sodas and then collect the bottles and return them to the cafeteria, earning $0.25 Dominican pesos each. I needed to return enough bottles to buy at least one Nutella sachet the following day, or to indulge at kermesses (field days) and school bake sales. It wasn't that the lunch my mom packed for me was not enough; I was just willing to "work" to afford my guilty pleasures.

Fast forward to today. It's that time of the month when we start getting e-statements and payment due alerts, and all our toiletries are empty. I spent the last week preparing to file my taxes. Tomorrow I am meeting with the accountant. For the last few years, this appointment has felt more like going to the confessional. Naked. Guilty. This time I will confess to you, too.

The girl who used to find household budgets on yellowed napkins and still marvels at how her mother managed to cover braces and ballet with a Dominican schoolteacher salary; the girl who worked and saved for every single need she had, from shoes to moving abroad; the girl who opened high-yield savings accounts and her first IRA at twenty-four— that girl would not believe where I am today.

I am in huge debt.

HUGE.

My debt is at an all-time high, and my credit score an all-time low. Almost daily, I wake up to emails about my checking account being overdrawn. All of my credit cards are maxed out. Don't even ask me about savings. What savings?

I still remember most of the personal finance lessons I learned from newspapers, magazines, TV, radio, and websites. Information seemed to be everywhere during the 2008 financial crisis—even though the crisis didn't affect me much because I had and kept a good-paying job during that time. I made the most of my weekly allowance, and I was the Queen of Freelancing. The trick is keeping fixed expenses low and being proactive, creative, frugal, and a minimalist when necessary. You also have to put yourself out there: You can't be broke and shy at the same time! But I still fell into debt. I guess I got lost somewhere in the middle, and then I couldn't find my way back.

I have been in debt before. Not this much, though. I borrowed money from my mom to buy my first used car in the US. I paid in cash. And I paid her back quickly. Two years later, in our mother-daughter version of a student loan, she lent me money to pay for my online master's degree. Again, I paid her back as quickly as I could. A year after that, she helped me with a large down payment for my first brand new car. That time I took a while to pay her back, even though I had saved the money (I spent it and then had to save it again). She never charged me interest: Borrowing from my mom was always a great deal.

These days I have bad debt and good debt as a result of:

+ "luxuries" such as not taking much work while pregnant
+ expensive, self-paid health insurance and medical care
+ an embarrassing chain of not-the-smartest financial moves in my household
+ another professional certification tuition
+ two big dental emergencies
+ one mortgage

Long story short: I lived beyond my means during periods of not working up to my full potential. Downsizing and relocating to Nicaragua helped, but many of the items we needed were much more expensive there, and with the added costs of constant travel, we just couldn't keep up. The current financial system doesn't help much, but today, I promise you and myself that I will get out of this. I will never put myself in this sickening situation again. I have worked too hard and too long for most of my adult life—I can't afford to be stressed about money anymore.

I believe in working to increase our means. Working to afford what's important to us. I am not talking about building a fortune. We just need enough. What is enough? What was enough before? What is enough now? Enough to be and feel free. At least debt free. Enough to live and share, which means separating our wants and perceived needs from what's essential.

How much does it cost to be a woman in her thirties in the United States? What about in other parts of the world? Basic food and water, healthcare, education, shelter, clothing, retirement? In some cases, add maternity and childcare. Plus longevity is in my genes. So along with everything else, I worry about outliving my savings. Being alive should never be a financial death penalty.

I will invest in myself to get there. That is always the responsible thing to do, but especially now that I am a mother. I deserve to have enough to afford a lifestyle that brings peace of mind to my family and me.

We need so little to be happy, if we can just make that choice. My mantras these days: Experiences before things. Presence instead of presents. Well-lived time is the real currency, happiness is the real wealth.

For everything else, there is great advice from my favorite financial coach, Sandra Acosta.

Because I am an economist who has worked in numerous treasury departments, managing the money of big corporations, most people think I have an automatic advantage when it comes to managing my own finances. Well, no, that is not how it works.

For the longest time, I thought I knew what I was doing with my income. I had a spreadsheet with all my expenses clearly listed, and if I had room for one more, I would just add it to the list. After all, what is one additional small monthly payment, right?

On the other hand, I have always wanted to be financially independent and have my own successful business. I was positive that it was going to happen "someday" by "magic." I know, ridiculous.

I knew that I was not going to achieve financial independence through my salary, so my ears were open to investment opportunities. In the early 2000s, a friend of mine told me about an opportunity to buy land. I listened to her, and just like that—with my eyes closed—I proceeded to buy a few lots. Then I forgot about them for a couple years, but I made sure I paid their taxes on time. That was all I had to do.

I was living in Coral Springs, Florida when I landed a job in the Brickell neighborhood of downtown Miami. You can only imagine what my commute was like (forty-eight miles each way). Brickell was surging at that time, and condos were going up left and right. Well, I was getting tired of all that driving and started thinking about moving to Miami to be closer to work. I would save so much gas and time every day. Lucky me: My net worth was high because the lots I had bought were six or seven times what I paid for them. So I sold them right away and used the money for a down payment on a brand new condo. I thought I had hit the jackpot.

I was far from correct. I had been talked into a mortgage with variable interest, understanding that within a few years, I could refinance to a traditional mortgage.

I was convinced I had made it and that I only needed to repeat the process. Within a few months of closing, I was approved for a home equity line. For the record, I did not go crazy and buy shoes or a new car or anything like that. I bought more land. Smart, right?

Between 2007 and 2008, when world markets went downhill, I also hit rock bottom. I lost my condo and my land was worth pennies. Oh, and I had zero as an emergency fund.

Let's talk credit cards. Consumer debt is the biggest and most dangerous epidemic out there. I know, I know, you feel "the love." Credit card companies reward you and give you miles, points, and 0 percent interest for a few months. I will give you one tip: If you cannot pay 100 percent of what you buy each month, you cannot afford it and you should not buy it. Simple.

I found myself digging a deep hole. I was hypnotized by the 0 percent interest deal. Yes, I would plan to pay the card off quickly, but then with every paycheck came some unexpected expense, and I would have to direct my cash elsewhere. At the end of those few months, of course, interest rates skyrocketed, and I ended up paying absurd amounts of extra money for items that were not worth it. Full disclosure: I am still in debt but close to paying it off. Within two years, I will be free. I used to be ashamed of my situation, but someone very important in the personal finance field told me this in regard to debt and paying it off: "You are going to gain so much strength and resolve and focus from the practice of paying down your credit card debt, and that is going to make you even more badass at growing your investments and reaching financial freedom." So not all is bad. By crushing our debt, we are cementing extraordinary habits to get to the next level.

You may be able to win the credit card game by paying the balance in full every month and taking advantage of rewards and points, but you need the kind of discipline that keeps you in the gym the entire year, not just January. Know yourself.

Who did I have to blame for all this chaos? Me. I made all these "smart" investments without doing any research. Without analyzing different scenarios and without any kind of cash in reserve. Who in the world does that? Well, if I want to make myself feel better, I can look around and see I am not the only one. Most Americans cannot come up with $400 to cover an emergency. We need to make educated decisions. We need to read, learn, and listen to success stories. Just because most people live like this doesn't make it right.

We cannot look around, see a "normal" lifestyle, be okay with it, and get comfortable. We are not going to change the education system, but we all can do our part in learning and transmitting important information to others. There is no shortage of content about finance.

The point of all this chaos was for me to learn that I am the one responsible for my destiny. It all comes down to that. I cannot blame anyone for the good or the bad that comes out of my actions.

When I finally started reading about finance, I realized that it is about a lot more than making money: it is about becoming a better version of me. I changed my mindset. Because if I were going to make more money with the same mindset, I'd end up in the same place.

One big lesson was to grow up and accept the fact that I wouldn't be financially independent "someday" by "magic." I had to start working toward that goal. Nobody was going to hand it to me. Listen, nobody is going to hand you your goals, either. Go after them yourself.

We all have different areas we want to develop and improve. We all want to travel, spend time with family, be healthy, workout, celebrate with friends. Well, as much as you read about what to eat and not eat, how to exercise, and where to spend your next vacation, you also need to study personal finance. Don't accept financial matters as your weakness. People will say, "I'm a designer, I'm a nurse, I'm a teacher. Therefore, I am not good with money." Stop it.

It's easier than ever to take control of your finances, and on top of that, you do not need a lot of money to start saving and investing.

The first thing you need to learn is how to *live with 90 percent of your income*. I am positive you will find expenses in your monthly bank statement that you do not even remember because they're on automatic debit. How about automatic savings? The amount does not matter, just start now. Don't wait for the perfect scenario. My advice: do not save just to save. Have a purpose, give a name to that savings account. Disney trip in a year. New furniture for our patio in six months, etc.

Do not increase your fixed expenses. That is, do not play the lifestyle inflation game. This happens when your spending increases with your income. It happens to everyone who is not paying attention. So next time you receive a raise for any reason, keep your same spending level, and save and invest the difference. You already know how to live with a lower income.

Clarity is key. You need to know what you want and say no to everything else. What is the dream that gives you joy? Do not go to Disney World because everybody else goes. Go to Disney World because you cannot wait to have a picture with Mickey.

Write down your goals. I do this on a daily basis thanks to Brian Tracy. I have them divided by Business and Career, Finance, Intimate Relationships, Family and Friends, Personal Growth, Health and Fitness, Contribution, Spirituality, and Fun and Recreation. This way I can keep balance and work on all aspects of my life.

With goals in hand, you can now direct your money to what really matters to you. This is when you become the master and tell your money what to do, not the other way around. Please include building an emergency fund in your goals so you can pay off any debt. An emergency fund is a cushion you have when something goes wrong and helps you avoid the use of credit cards to cover the unexpected. Experts recommend having between six and twelve months of living expenses in a savings account, available for emergencies only. Do not get overwhelmed by the number. Just get it done. If you do not have any savings at the moment, start doing the math. Come up with your number and break it down into smaller goals. I recently recognized the importance of an emergency fund. I wanted to rush into investing and have every cent working for me, but that changed when I saw more than seventy people laid off in one day.

What if that would have been me?

Once you have clarity, you need to *focus and go crush those goals*. This process will make your creativity spike as you find ways to save more, eliminate unnecessary expenses, and have a side hustle. I decided to earn some extra money by teaching Zumba®. I love, love, love, teaching Zumba®. That is one big positive about side hustles. You get paid to do what you love. It is kind of like getting paid for having a hobby. Do you love dogs? Get hired to walk them. How about baking? Or hand-lettering cards? Guess what? Now you have extra money to put to work, to invest.

Always create ways to *diversify your income*. It should not be coming from one stream only. There are different ways to do this. Start your research and start investing. No excuses.

Having control of your finances means a lot more than taking care of money. When you *change your mindset,* you see every aspect of your life with different eyes. It is powerful.

Now that you are in your thirties, you should be saving and investing for your future self. Nobody is going to rescue you. *If your company offers a 401K, sign up. If not, open an IRA and start contributing now.* Get involved, it is your future we are talking about. Read books, listen to experts, hire a financial coach. There is no one-size-fits-all solution. There is no magical formula to follow and be financially free. Every person has a different story, and unique circumstances that need to be addressed with a customized plan. Working with a financial professional provides accountability and reminds you that you are not alone.

—— **SANDRA ACOSTA** is an economist who earned her degree at Universidad Externado de Colombia. After a successful career as a treasury analyst, financial advisor, and fitness entrepreneur, Sandra now shares her expertise as a financial coach. Her vast resume includes prestigious institutions such as Ocean Bank, Florida International University, April USA Assistance, Norwegian Cruise Line, Prestige Cruise Holdings, Warner Channel, and Morgan Stanley.

– *Living* –

I was in line to pay at Carter's one afternoon when I saw a photocopied flyer announcing a casting. The company was looking for clothing models, both babies and kids. "All ethnicities and special needs welcome!" the ad said. Underneath was a request for two current photos. Money was tight at the time, and the pay was listed as "good/high." I thought I should at least send recent pictures of Luca. Maybe we could earn some extra cash, and it might even be fun.

I ran the idea by Claudio. "Where are they making those clothes?" he asked me. I said I didn't know. "What if they're from sweatshops?" he said. I looked down at Luca and decided right then and there that we would find another way to earn money. I didn't want my infant to support a business that may have been profiting off cheap foreign labor.

Something similar happened when we set out to buy our first family Christmas tree. We wanted a big, live tree. I saw that Home Depot was selling them for $100 each. Claudio thought about it and then suggested that we buy from the Mexican seller down the street. He was our neighbor, and he needed the money more than any big retail chain.

These are choices we have the privilege of making: decisions and habits, a sense of awareness about the impact of our actions, the personal culture that we live by and share with the world. It's the opposite of the glam, fast fashion, happy hour ritual of my twenties. Back then every day had its purpose. Mondays were Reggae night at Purdy's. On Wednesdays you could find me enjoying live music at Uva on Ponce de Leon. And Saturdays? Saturdays were designed specifically for shopping! The one thing I did every day was talk to friends on the phone for hours. Our favorite topic? Men.

I'm not saying life in my twenties wasn't fun—at the time. I finally had the spending power to enjoy flexible work, a gym membership, an active social life, and world travel. And I did it all with *chispa*, just like when I used to smile way too hard in family pictures. I was a natural at finding positivity in the midst of chaos.

But life kept changing and challenging me, like it does to all of us. I started to see that the choices I was making weren't leading to much wisdom, substance, or depth. I was basically on a work-play hamster wheel. And then I experienced a health crisis. All of my lifestyle choices suddenly came down to health because I had to change almost everything I was doing. I learned that committing to taking care of our health is the ultimate act of love toward our loved ones and ourselves. It's a lesson I keep learning every day.

Once I arrived in Nicaragua, I started to think even more about how my actions made me feel. I didn't like how gossiping felt, so I stopped. Eating clean food meant I was taking care of my health, so that became my diet. Though daily life came with all kinds of difficulties, I looked at this new country and decided to be a force for good.

Along the way I'd hear some feedback that encouraged me. My dear cousin Marco read my post about how amazed I am at the fact that I have worn dental retainers for thirty years straight. "Something I admire about you is your clarity before commitments," he wrote to me, "your willingness to accept commitment. These are difficult things that require commitment and you face them voluntarily. Many things happen to people, but not many people make things happen."

I had never thought of myself in terms of clarity or commitment, other than when it came to Claudio. But it turned out that those were qualities I possessed and could continue to develop. The simple act of telling someone how you see them can be transformative. If you've moved away from home, committed to a long-distance relationship, or taken charge of your health, you're also making things happen for yourself. Cheers to us!

My nephew, Ian, now calls me eco-tía because I avoid using plastic bags, and I'm known for teaching him yoga stretches after his baseball practice. When he comes over to my house, he eats pastured eggs and multigrain avocado toast. I know I'm breaking the bank with organic and local products, but it's a choice I make for my family and for the environment. It doesn't work for everyone, but it works for us, even if my dentist rolls her eyes when I tell her I've switched to natural toothpaste.

We all have our own unique evolution. We find out—hopefully sooner rather than later—what works for us and try to live accordingly. Just the other day I saw the mother of one of Luca's little friends jogging with her stroller in our neighborhood. She'd given birth only a few weeks earlier. "Good for you," I said. "It's been two years and I still haven't started working out."

"Oh no, it's part of my lifestyle," she said. For her it was normal to go back to exercising. I liked how she said it with such certainty. She knew exactly what she needed.

My conversations with friends have shifted, too. We don't talk about men that much these days (though they show up from time to time). Now we discuss eco-cleaning products—I consider myself the resident expert—exfoliating with avocado peels, our next steps for our careers, and how to improve our relationships not only with our partners, but with ourselves.

I am far from perfect. I make mistakes and slip back into old patterns all the time. But I also know that lifestyle is the category in which I've experienced the most change during my thirties. Even this essay changed dramatically. The first draft was so easy for me to write, if you could say that about any section of this book. Years later, when I read it over again, I felt there was so much more to say because of how much our lifestyles change in our thirties. My goal is no longer a constant search for happiness and pleasure; now it's well-being. In every part of my life, from relationships to finances, health to community, I've noticed a clear shift toward seeking wisdom and consciousness that I'd like to develop as much as possible. These are the questions I ask myself when I need a tune-up:

Am I making positive choices or negative choices?
Am I building myself up or knocking myself down?
What do I notice: the good or the bad?
Where do I focus: on myself or on others?
What do I do with my pain: destroy or create?
Is there alignment between my beliefs, my values, and my actions?

We all have our own questions and goals, and the choices we make lead us in different directions. I'm trying my best to be more aware, because I've learned that answers come in mysterious forms, and new questions emerge every day. It helps to have a guide, which is why I talked to Dashama Konah about how we can consciously choose and evolve our lifestyles while also considering their impact on the world.

Did you have any major breakthroughs in life as you approached your thirties, or now that you are in your thirties?

I have breakthroughs all the time! Now that I am in my thirties, they are becoming subtler and more exciting instead of being so healing and earth shattering like they were in my twenties. One big breakthrough for me was the manifestation of my travel TV show. I worked toward creating this show for several years after being in the top 1 percent out of twenty thousand auditions to have my own show on the Oprah Winfrey Network. We filmed the first episode in Bali!

How did you get interested in the fields of lifestyle coaching and sustainability?

I have always lived according to the sustainability practices I teach, so it was a natural direction for me. People would come to me for coaching even in high school, so it made sense to finally become a professional. It's what I am most passionate about and I love what I do.

What is your background in these areas?

I have traveled the world teaching yoga and holistic lifestyle for over fifteen years, transforming millions of people globally. I was initially a certified fitness trainer, consulting for hospitals, schools, and businesses, as well as country clubs, studios, and gyms. I then trained as a yoga teacher and nutrition coach, and have studied Neuro-Linguistic Programming, Thai yoga therapy, martial arts, Qi gong, and many other healing modalities. I combined the best of all of these to create the fusion system I call the Prasha Method and Pranashama Yoga.

What are the components of an ideal and sustainable lifestyle?

Conscious choice-making and practicing awareness around each decision is at the root of this ideal. We have so many choices for food, clothing, products, services, home, cars, activities, and experiences. Each of these aspects of our lifestyle includes choices that can have a negative, positive, or neutral impact on our earth, and the positive choices are the sustainable ones—those that contribute to the continuation of our ecosystems and the nourishment of our bodies and the environment, and impact the world around us in a progressive, positive way.

How does our lifestyle affect our relationships, health, spirituality, career, and finances?

We typically attract people who have lifestyles and views similar to our own. So this is a huge component of who we attract, the opportunities, career, and relationships we seek, and the financial success (or lack thereof) that we experience. My philosophy is: "What we focus on expands," "We attract what we are or what we need to grow," and "Everything is a message."

How do addictions impact us, our loved ones, and our life in general?

Addictions typically lead to suffering. They can be damaging, and even devastating. When we become aware of addictions and consciously choose to overcome them (by getting help or just quitting cold turkey), we demonstrate to ourselves and others self-love and respect for our life and theirs.

Any tips for stress-free time management?

Plan ahead, be organized, don't sweat the small stuff, don't try to do too much at once, don't multitask if you can avoid it, be present for whomever you are with, and be kind to yourself and others—you get a lot further along in achieving your goals that way.

How can we develop the habit of positive thinking?

If it is not already a habit, it can be learned. You can start with writing positive affirmations, writing "I am" statements. Then take the work into the mirror and look into your own eyes and say it. Be grateful for even the smallest things in your life. Meditate on love and happiness daily. Practice smiling even if you're not happy.

How can we have a better attitude toward the issues of everyday life?

Be grateful and realize there are so many others far worse off than you are.

What is your key piece of advice for achieving a sustainable and positive lifestyle that leads to higher personal development?

The key to achieving a sustainable and positive lifestyle is to take it one moment at a time. Be mindful of each and every choice and decision from what you eat to what you think, say, and do. These all combine to weave the fabric of the magical life you are creating. One of my favorite quotes by Aristotle is, "We are what we repeatedly do. Excellence, then, is not an act, but a habit." One decision won't create a sustainable, healthy life, but consistent daily decisions and choices will, over time, and you will marvel at the beautiful life you have created as you look back and see that each choice has led you to where you are now. What choices will you make today that will lead you to who you aspire to become?

—— **DASHAMA KONAH** is an internationally known author, life and business strategist, speaker, producer, and yoga teacher. A media favorite, Dashama has been featured on ABC, NBC, FOX News, Discovery, and Oprah.com, as well as in *Cosmo Magazine*, *Teen Vogue*, *The Wall Street Journal*, and *Forbes*. She has spoken at events in many countries and at the United Nations, University of Virginia, Warwick Business School, and Sony Motion Picture Studios. With a degree in international business and communication, she has been a spirit-driven entrepreneur consulting for and creating international brands and businesses for over fifteen years. She teaches that the power of the mind, discipline, and positive intention are the greatest influences on your conscious evolution and success.

III

Back To Basics

When Claudio and I arrived in Granada, Nicaragua, we moved into a small room at the back of a cigar factory called Mombacho. It was more glamorous than it sounds. In Nicaragua, a factory can be anywhere with a table and a few chairs. The expertly trained cigar rollers at our factory worked at a table in the front of a spacious colonial home that had an inner courtyard with a pool and red jungle geraniums (the same flowers we would offer to *La Virgen de La Altagracia* in Higüey, my mom's hometown).

Lisette, Mombacho's staff cook, housekeeper, and all around lifesaver, prepared lunch every day for the workers, and when the food was ready, I would take a break from my computer and help her serve dozens of plates filled with white rice, refried beans seasoned with Worcestershire sauce, pickled cabbage slaw, fried plantains, meatballs, fish, and tortillas.

Sometimes Claudio would cook Italian meals adapted to local ingredients, such as penne with Dos Pinos cream and *mercado* vegetables. Some of the Nicas loved Claudio's food, others not so much. I tried my hand with *mofongo,* a classic Dominican dish of fried plantains mashed with *chicharrón* (fried pork skin). They were crazy about it, but kept mentioning how expensive the dish was. I had not realized that *chicharrón* was a delicacy in Nicaragua.

Though I still missed our life in Miami, I was quickly falling in love with the peace and tranquility I found in Nicaragua. This was the first time in my life that I was simply being, simply living in the present, and with almost no technology. No smartphone, no car, no apartment, no nine-to-five job, and so many free hours to enjoy the movies, magazines, and websites I'd put off for years. I slept soundly every night in our tiny room with wood paneling, our suitcases tucked under the bed. I walked through the city as a tourist, reporting my findings to Claudio at night as we sprayed ourselves with citronella and dined under the stars: the *vigorón* stand at the *parque central,* an old man carrying flowers on his head while riding his bike past the main cathedral, the pale blue of Lago Cocibolca in the early morning, the elegant horse-drawn funeral processions, men giving rides to women on the modified bars of their bikes while texting, tourists discovering the city through the lenses of their cellphones, a woman walking the streets and singing out her inventory of produce: *Piña! Papaya! Sandía!*

We visited Granada once before Claudio accepted the job. We swam in Laguna de Apoyo, watched the sunset in *las isletas* as howler monkeys jumped from tree to tree. We sailed around Mombacho volcano with its jagged top capped in mist. I climbed the bell tower of a 500-year-old church to see the city from above—the red tiled roofs, the old colonial streets, motorbikes, exhaust, church bells, markets. I sat next to Claudio in a 1974 red Toyota Land Cruiser convertible as we drove down dark jungle roads. When Mombacho hosted its annual party, I was the only new person in the mix. They called happy hour "18 Time" for the Flor de Caña Centenario 18 rum they drank every night. I wore a white tank top and white shorts, puffed a cigar carefully, and danced salsa on the terrace. Claudio got in the pool first and then signaled to his new business partners, who promptly picked me up and tossed me in. My straight hair was ruined for the rest of the trip, but I was happy. Claudio was, too. We made our decision and never looked back.

I didn't know much about Nicaragua before moving there. I'd met a Nicaraguan in Venezuela, and I had my friend Leana in Miami. I knew the strong smell of the reused frying oil from the *fritangas* in Sweetwater, Florida, where many Nicas live, and of course I'd always known that *gallo pinto* with eggs and cheese makes a perfect meal, and that Luis Enrique, a proud Nicaraguan, was a world-class salsa singer. But I didn't expect the mix of indigenous faces and classic Spanish names. I was surprised to learn that Nicas celebrate Santo Domingo as a saint, that the country is filled with green valleys in between the famous lakes and volcanoes. I never thought that one day I would be personally grateful for Mombacho, the massive volcano that inspired the name of Claudio's company and erupted in 1570 but never toppled.

Being in a touristic city, I thought I could offer public relations services to hotels. I found out quickly that the tourism industry was still undeveloped in Granada and the rest of Nicaragua at that time. Local businesses were fighting to survive. Few of them had the time or money to hire someone. There was an occasional entertainment event in Managua, but nothing like what we'd had in the Dominican Republic or the States. Many of the television programs and newspaper articles came from international networks and news agencies. It was canned content, and what was original was highly censored, with the exception of a few courageous media outlets. The Nicaraguans were just starting to write their stories following the 1972 earthquake and the Somoza dictatorship.

Meanwhile, Claudio had the job of his dreams. I could see it in his face, a newfound happiness and sense of accomplishment that helped him regain his identity. He'd gone through an extremely thorough hiring process, including a Sunday morning interview after a Saturday night of serious Oktoberfest partying. The offer from Mombacho was an answer to his prayers (*"Gesú, Giuseppe e Maria: Fattemi avere una tabaccheria"*). This role had more responsibilities than any of his previous jobs, and he was up to the challenge. I watched him blending new cigars, searching for tobacco leaves from suppliers in Estelí (the capital of Nicaraguan tobacco), Jalapa, and Honduras, recruiting the staff of *boncheros* and *roleras*, negotiating with box makers and ring designers, maintaining the cigar supply during the six-month rainy season in our home factory with its leaky roof, even giving tours in Spanish, English, Italian, and French. I was proud to see him grow as a professional and as a man.

At first I wasn't looking for friends. In my mind I still had my old life, which I'd only put on pause. I had Skype dates with friends and family abroad, and real dates with Claudio on nights and weekends. Our house was always filled with people. Sometimes I'd meet a solo female traveler at a yoga class. We might grab coffee or share a meal, but people in Granada were always passing through. At least in the beginning, that was my goal too. Our plan was to be there for one year, save, and then come back to the States.

Claudio and I were atypical expats. We couldn't relate to many of the classic expat struggles and triumphs. We spoke the language. We were both Latino, accustomed to the heat and bugs from years of living in the tropics. We didn't explore much—Claudio's schedule didn't allow it and maybe we weren't that curious. We didn't join poker games, Frisbee groups, or book clubs. People at home kept asking me: "Have you made friends?" Eventually I realized I hadn't.

One night I was locked out of our house and happened to meet a young woman who lived next door—Malena from Puebla, Mexico. She and her partner were opening a new café that would soon become my headquarters. Miraculously, in a city filled with mostly retired expats, I had somehow found an expat couple our age.

Malena became my first friend in Granada, and what a great one. She opened her doors to me and I opened mine to her. We listened to each other, helped each other, supported each other, comforted each other, and gave each other "therapy." We talked about everything and everyone, our version of small-town gossip. Life was sometimes difficult, but we also found beauty and happiness all around us. I jumped in her car every time she went to Managua to buy supplies for her café. I brought packages for her from the States, and her in-laws brought me supplements from Canada for my HPV treatment. I helped her translate and copyedit her menu. I set up her TripAdvisor account and we celebrated each glowing review. She cooked *mole poblano* for Claudio and me. We recommended each other for every available opportunity in Nicaragua, brainstormed business ideas, introduced each other to our few acquaintances at the time. We even visited Mexico together when I was working on a show there one summer. I was so proud to introduce Malena to her country's capital for the first time, and not at all surprised by her production talents when she filled in last minute on the show. Malena changed and saved my life.

Because of Malena, I met Amy, a fellow production coordinator, writer, yoga instructor, digital nomad, and dancer at heart. She was in Nicaragua teaching, writing, and collaborating with La Escuela de la Comedia y el Mimo, a nonprofit theatrical school for at-risk youth in Granada. Her writing advice became my new motto: "Never work too hard on something that is not your book!"

Sometimes we'd meet in the local gym's spinning room to have *Sex and the City*-style catch up dates. We'd search for the two almost-comfortable bikes and then start in on another session. The gym was in an open-air colonial home—no air conditioning, just a few small oscillating fans. It wasn't as glamorous as Manhattan, but glamour wasn't the point. We had things to talk about: where to find the best (and cheapest!) almonds and pumpkin seeds, how to cook alkalizing recipes with local ingredients, hormone issues that had arisen in our early thirties, the pain and joy of writing, how to line dry your clothes during the rainy season, first world problems and nostalgia, especially for Whole Foods and Walgreens, and of course: men. We wondered what we really needed to live and thrive.

We got along without so many basics like dependable water and electricity. Sometimes it felt like we'd freed ourselves of a huge burden. Other times it felt like we were giving up way too much.

Nicaraguans would often wonder where I was from. Some of them thought I was from the Atlantic Coast because I'm dark-skinned with curly hair like the *costeños*. Every now and then I was mistaken for a Nica, especially at landmarks and museums that I'd visit often with our guests. The local staff thought I was a tour guide and offered me the rate for nationals. But I resisted—I was uncomfortable with the idea. I am too proud of a Dominican to pass for anything else, plus I was okay with paying the tourist rate.

In the States, most people had met a Dominican before. There was an existing stereotype for Dominicans, our women, slang, dances, music, and food. In Miami I saw the Dominican flag here and there. Nicaragua was the exact opposite. I was well aware that I was representing my country and that I was one of only a few Dominicans the locals were likely to meet. I held on to my Dominican accent. I had given up a lot to be in Nicaragua, so I tried to keep what cultural heritage I still had. Out of respect and gratitude for the locals, I eventually called myself "Domi-Nican."

I started writing this book two weeks after I landed in Granada. It was a challenge, getting used to working on my own, managing my time, dealing with the heat, finding the motivation in such a laid back environment—and finding a chair that I could sit in for more than an hour. Eventually I walked to Gonper, the one local office supply store, to buy an imported office chair (not cheap in Nicaragua). At night, Claudio would roll my chair to the side of the pool, take a seat, and lean back to see the stars overhead. We fought over who got the office chair at every dinner.

I turned thirty-one, then thirty-two, then thirty-three, and the town began to feel smaller and smaller. I felt like I was living on *The Truman Show*: my coordinates were the lake, our home street, the street with the local gym, and the cathedral. The boundaries of Granada were tightening. I used maps and TripAdvisor reviews, like all the other anonymous tourists. Some days I felt completely invisible.

I could always see beauty and hope in Granada and the Nicaraguans, but I also saw so many of the sad Dominican images that I grew up with and ultimately ran away from. I had forgotten about the challenges people face in the third world: kids selling chewing gum to tourists at night, men catcalling women on every corner, street dogs roaming the parks, elderly people selling homemade desserts in the midday heat. If you walked just outside of the city center, you saw another world. There the water didn't run for days on end, despite the fact that one of the biggest lakes in the world was just a few blocks away. Just like in the Dominican Republic, dengue plagued these neighborhoods. Theft was rampant. People were desperate. Yet you could always hear the sounds of worship, whether they were coming from the cathedrals or the Evangelical churches, which had lively gatherings every Friday night.

The Nicaraguans had a kind of calm detachment. Many of them hadn't had the opportunity to get an education. They weren't natural leaders. They sometimes felt powerless because they had been victims for so much of their national history, either in the hands of a cruel dictator or in the aftermath of devastating earthquakes. Xochilt, one of the Mombacho cigar rollers, used to tell me: "Nicaraguans are just happy to eat." One time I heard Doneyda, another Mombacho staff member, commenting on some questionable leftovers in the refrigerator: "I'd rather eat it and get sick than throw it away and waste it," she said, which was the exact opposite of what my mom had taught me. Nicaraguans sought food, water, shelter, clothing. They had to focus on the basics.

I hated myself for complaining, but at the same time I couldn't find the food staples I needed for my health. I was trying to follow an anti-inflammatory, alkaline diet to keep my HPV infection at bay and my hormones balanced, but without the right ingredients. I marveled at my strong immune system but worried about my health, the way my stomach sometimes reacted to the local food, and then there was dengue, chikungunya, Zika. I breathed in smoke whenever my neighbors burned their garbage. I didn't think I was better than my surroundings; I was just trying to heal.

Questions kept arising: Would we ever save enough money to go back to the US? Would we live in Granada forever? Would we have kids? Where would we raise them? Were we happy? Was I living my own life? Would I ever work full-time again? And what type of work should I do? Was it worth it to keep paying for the storage unit in Miami? The answer to that last question was no, but of course we kept paying anyway. After I had entered the country multiple times, the Nica immigration agents started asking about the purpose of my trip. I wondered the same thing. I was visiting my husband, dreaming up new lives and possibilities while also feeling incredibly frustrated. I tried on different job titles: Production Manager, Communications Expert, Writer. None seemed to suit me. For the first time in my adult life I was financially dependent on someone else, and I didn't like that feeling at all.

Our first year in Nicaragua gave us a break from the stress of Miami—it was a grace period— but then Nica became a strong force in our lives, a character in our trials. We stayed years longer than planned because we hadn't saved up enough money to buy a house. Claudio was enjoying his job, but he couldn't find someone he could trust to be in charge, so if he left, everything he built would fall apart. He also started having doubts— about Miami, children, our marriage. In my own mind, I told myself that the day I got pregnant, I would fly back to the States. But I didn't get pregnant. All of this took a huge toll on our marriage and the inevitable hurt showed up, unwanted but urgent. I was shaken to my core. I was overwhelmed, neglected, and frustrated as a woman, professional, and wife. I experienced in real life some of my worst nightmares: excess, lack of commitment, the wrong priorities, immaturity, uncertainty, disrespect. Claudio and I hurt each other in our own ways. After one of our worst fights, I lost my wedding ring while riding in a taxi in

Managua. It felt like a sign. I remember when I started looking at him differently. My eyes and the expression on my face didn't match the feelings in my heart. We confronted our worst fears: fear of the people we had become, fear of losing each other, fear that one day it would be too much and too late. I cried, prayed, and cried again. But strangely, all of this made me feel more positive about our potential as partners. Our concerns were a reflection of how responsible we actually were, and what a strong foundation we wanted for our family. Now I can see that, spiritually, we weren't done with Nica. It had more to teach us.

One day I came across Jim Rohn's famous quote: "You are the average of the five people you spend the most time with." I had heard it before, but I'd never taken the time to think about who those five people were in my life. I had more than five in Santo Domingo and Miami—but not in Granada. My circle there was way too small, and that needed to change. I started approaching women in town at their businesses, the gym, on the street. Some of them had mentioned their desire for "girl time," which we talked about but never acted on. Others were simply not interested. Then I learned that April, one sweet American woman who was a talented and dedicated trainer at the local gym during the day and an amazing vocalist/mouth trumpeter and salsa dancer at night, was stressed out about planning her wedding. I felt for her because I hadn't enjoyed my wedding planning either, but I did have my own experience plus my production experience. I offered to help. We met and I started working with her on the budget and connected her with local vendors I knew from Claudio's business events. After a few months, she opened her circle and introduced me to her friends, who happened to be the movers and shakers of Granada.

They were all hard-working women: managers, business owners, artists, creators, founders of the top businesses in town. They also had a workout club called BAMF. Their Facebook page description says it all: "This club is for all the Bad Ass Mujeres Fuertes in Nicaragua who like to get up way too early to kick ass together in the morning BEFORE THEIR MORNING COFFEE!!!" In the beginning, I couldn't even imagine waking up at 5 a.m. to workout at 5:30 a.m. at the local gym or outside Convento San Francisco. But I realized that if I wanted to hang out with these kinds of women, I would need to suck it up.

We would train hard and bond right after over tea or coffee, and then head home at 7:30 a.m. to start our productive days. This group shaped my body and my mind. It was inspiring to be surrounded by such strong-willed women. They were my local equivalent to Sheryl Sandberg, Arianna Huffington, and Oprah, and at that time in my life I needed all three. We were from different places, but we were united in one goal: celebrating our feminine power. I offered to host our first reading group, where we discussed *Women Who Run with the Wolves*. We tackled all topics with no judgment: depression, trauma, the solace and joys of the human experience, relationships, self-acceptance, self-love, denying ourselves, putting ourselves first, neglecting ourselves, challenging inertia, committing to deeper self-work. I realized that if I had met these women early on, my life in Granada would have been very different.

The BAMF crew motivated me to get out of my shell. I learned that I could simply be the friend I wanted to have, that I didn't have to wait for others to open up to me. I could start by reaching out. That's how I met Yudith, a talented Nica beauty specialist who did my waxing at the ChocoMuseo on Calle Atravesada. After she moved her business to a hotel in Laguna de Apoyo, outside the city center, she would come to my house for appointments. I cherished our conversations, most of which we had while I was at least half naked! She invited me to her wedding, and later on got pregnant five months after I did. I was able to share with her a beautiful pregnancy blouse, and also gave her prenatal yoga classes (though she was only able to take one class—she had her baby just a few days later). Yudith is now a spa room owner in Granada, and I proudly celebrate her success via Facebook. When I treated myself to a waxing appointment at her new place, she melted my heart when she showed me an issue of *NewBeauty Magazine* I had given her years ago. "I always told myself I was going to have this magazine for my clients at my own spa," she said, a huge smile on her face. "Everybody loves it!" And I love her.

I also met a teenager named Eliezer who spoke English and decided to hire him as my author's assistant. I still can't believe I gave myself that luxury, but he showed up at the right time, and I needed his help. He gave his first paycheck to the church as a gesture of gratitude, and through our work together, I tried my best to mentor him. I told him not to worry about the price of an iPhone, that he didn't need to succumb to American consumerism. What the world really needed was his passion and his message—and his talents as a singer and dancer. During our collaboration, Eliezer came out and embraced his new identity in a country where doing so meant taking a huge personal risk. I was grateful to have played some small part in his life.

Yes, it was still a difficult period in my own life—and Claudio's—but if I ever felt like complaining again, all I had to do was think of Andrea and Mauricio, the most resourceful couple I've ever met. Mauricio was a jack of all trades at Mombacho, from driver to carpenter to literally any job you could imagine. Andrea was a housekeeper, beauty stylist, nanny, and successful entrepreneur. They were the same age as Claudio and me, but had a very different life simply because they'd been born in Nicaragua. Andrea not only took care of her three children but also woke up at 4 a.m., walked to the bus station, took a bus to the Masaya market to buy fruits and vegetables, returned home, made fresh soup and juice, and sold it from the back of her bike in the extreme tropical heat. Talk about motivation and hard work. What I most admired about this couple was how they did everything with love. I used to look at them and think that if I could just find the right perspective, I could make it through anything.

After contemplating life apart, Claudio and I realized that life is better together. We decided that we could endure the pain it takes to move forward. He was the head and I was the heart. Together we chose love while fighting the impulse to make decisions based on conventional wisdom, pride, or misguided fantasies. We are still healing. We are still learning to take care of ourselves and of each other. As clichéd as it sounds, we are a work-in-progress with a lifetime contract. I'm grateful for having the mindfulness, self-awareness, imagination, will, and strength to look for and pick the right tools to deal with my pain. I am thankful for the love and support that came from the cherished usual suspects and some unexpected hearts. I am amazed at the healing power of simply being aware and being willing to give back. Even in our saddest moments, we can make somebody else happy and that in itself will make us happy in return. God is in the details. You can find wisdom wherever you look, and love can bear almost anything.

The next chapter of our story starts in Miami. The city that was our home is our home once again. The skyline has changed since we left. The empty buildings we used to see during the economic crisis are now full, and dozens more have been built. The population is even more diverse. Each Latin American crisis has resulted in a new community in Miami, either voluntarily formed or due to exile. There is officially more Spanish spoken here than English, even on the windows of classic American stores at the mall. I'm still a tourist, and I will always be. I still fall in love with the Magic City every time I discover a new side of it. It's like having fifteen years of first dates. And the truth is that in my heart, I never really left.

Our four years of sacrifice, hard work, and uncertainty paid off, and even though we hadn't saved much, Claudio and I managed to purchase a modest home in Miami Shores, a two-bedroom craftsman built in 1941. It's filled with natural light and even has a fireplace in the living room. In the back we have a small butterfly and hummingbird garden, and a dwarf mango tree grows on our patio. We bought the house at a great price and slept here the day we signed. It feels like home—that is, until the next adventure changes our plans!

Claudio likes to walk barefoot on the grass in our backyard, feeling the soil that is now our property. It's his version of the American Dream. And of course there is Luca running through the house early in the morning, adding energy and a lot of joy. I've taken him to Nicaragua three times since we moved back to the States. We explore Granada as tourists and outsiders. Most of my friends are gone now. After the violent uprisings in the spring of 2018, Granada and the whole country have changed. The Nicas are doing their best to cope—with grace, as they always do. Nicaragua will forever have a place in my heart. It marked me, just like the tack I stepped on in La Calzada the night before I left the country to move back to Miami. The places we call home shape us, and hopefully we shape them too.

I've changed my ideas about our thirties. I was always in such a hurry—to grow up, date, be an adult, find a job, establish myself in the US, achieve professional goals, and have the car/house/husband of my dreams. Life was a marathon: I never stopped running. I even hurried to have my child before perimenopause would steal the possibility from me. But now I realize he arrived at the perfect time. I hurried to finish this book, too, but I had to experience everything that happened over the past seven years in order to be able to write it. When you speed through life, you either crash, get a ticket, or get sick from the cortisol rush, and in the end you always come up against a stop sign or red light. Now, instead of hurrying, I wish time would stop. I'm reminded of a quote I keep seeing online lately: "You are never early, you are never late. You're always right on time." You can't compare yourself or your experiences to anyone else. There really is no reference. There is only your life, and what you make of it.

The thirties, it turns out, are just life. Just living and being willing to learn the lessons life gives you. You can't hack experience. Rather than focusing on what I can accomplish during my thirties, I now think more about wrapping myself around this decade, literally embracing it and experiencing it and devoting it to what matters most. When I was doing some of the original research for this book, I spoke with a therapist about typical experiences in our thirties. She urged me not to generalize or make broad statements about being thirty—or any age. She said there are no stereotypes, that each person, each life is different. I remember being a little disappointed at the time, wondering if the whole concept of my book made any sense. It did, I see now, because I was seeking information and trying to describe what my friends and I were going through. I had the right idea. Maybe the question wasn't framed correctly, but the search and every single experience—no matter how difficult—was more than worth it. As a result, I am less concerned with tracking decades and years, though I do use them for motivation. I see decades as timeframes for momentum and change. I do that with years, too. But the grand to-do lists? I gave them up and learned to embrace uncertainty. I try to think about solutions more than checklists. After all, God laughs at our plans. Coronavirus, anyone?

Turning thirty is not so much a "big deal," as I used to say when I was twenty-nine—it's a great deal. The real gift is just being alive, just having the time to collect experiences and hopefully change for the better. For me, the thirties meant stripping away the life I'd made in order to see things very clearly, sometimes painfully so. I experienced marriage, health, and financial crises at the same time. I did a lot of living! So did many of my friends. Along the way I realized that a person can have more than one message in life. I've accepted the fact that messages and priorities evolve, and that we can't go wrong as long as we're being honest and open.

There is so much more I want to explore. I'm working on all parts of myself: woman, mother, wife, professional, human being. I'm building a family, a business, and a community while continuously building myself. I'm doing my best to keep reaching out and making new connections, because people are always the most important. I still have so many questions, but I know the answers will only come from experience itself. I have three years left in my thirties. Who knows what discoveries lie ahead, what questions I'll be asking next, what the coming years will teach me about who I am and who I want to be?

Only time will tell how I write the rest. No matter where life takes me, I know I can find my way.

IV

In Our Thirties:

A COLLECTION OF STORIES FROM
AROUND THE WORLD

Letter to My Younger Self

ZANIA SALA
Thirty, Puerto Rican

Dear Little Zania,

Even though as a teenager you may feel like the weight of the world is on your shoulders, you must know that the best is yet to come. You are still very young and naïve, and that is good. You must let time give you gills and courage. You are strong and beautiful, and every decision you have made in the past, as well as those you will make in the future, will shape you in unimaginable ways. I wish for you to be happy and free. So for that, I give you the following words of advice:

Congratulations on being such a responsible and disciplined student. Those two traits will get you very far in life, especially during your twenties, but they will also be your downfall. You will work tirelessly, and you will soon figure out that you cannot work without a purpose. In order to have a purpose you need to live with purpose. You may not know what it is now, but you will find out. Time will grant you that gift.

Keep saving your money. You won't always manage it correctly, but for the most part, you will be frugal and wise with it. In fact, you are so good with money that you will help others learn the value behind it. If you live within your means, everything will be alright.

Don't search for love in those who can't return the emotion. Love will find you unexpectedly, and it will be the kind of love that you never imagined existed. It's truthful, pure, imperfect, effortless, real, and incapable of harm. It might just be under your nose. Just remember, if you want to experience love at its highest level, you must surrender to the emotion when it comes to greet you.

It's okay to break the rules every once in a while. And guess what? You will, all in good faith. Know that some rules don't apply to you and are okay to break. No rulebook is intended to be one-size-fits-all. You will take risks in life that will scare you, but they will all be worth it in the end. You'll be fine.

Zania, you will discover that music is not your life. You will figure out that the reason for your voice is that you have one. Your voice is your instrument for conveying a message of hope and service. You will inspire through your voice, whether in song or not.

You don't need to prove to anyone that you are an artist. You just are. In fact, you don't need to prove anything to anyone. Don't sing because you are told to. Sing because you want to. Sing because you are happy and it makes you feel good. That will make all the difference.

You know how you've already picked family weekends at the beach over parties or staying over at friends' houses? That doesn't change. To you, family always comes first. Nature is also the reason why you love the water, wind, and sun so much. It feeds you. It speaks to you. It syncs with you. Go out into nature when you need to recharge. All you need to do is look outside.

Don't be so worried about what the future will bring. It's okay to prepare and plan ahead, but don't try to think too far ahead, because the horizon gets blurry. Some things are better left unknown. Experience will light your way. You have your feet on the ground and a good head on your shoulders. Don't be so hard on yourself, and don't give up.

Your love for your brothers remains like a steel chain. Help them out and ask them about their lives. Get them to talk to you. They look up to you, and you should open up to them. Together, you have an unbreakable bond that will last a lifetime. Be vulnerable with them. You will only benefit from it.

Know that you are very much like your parents. Both of them. Don't ever deny that. They have taught you well, and because of them, you will grow up to be self-reliant and filled with love. Make sure to hug them and let them know how much they mean to you. Love them as they have loved you.

Know that the love of your life is alive and unknowingly waiting for you. He is tall, handsome, smart, and sensible. He makes you a better woman and he doesn't judge you. He loves you, respects you, and supports you. He will fight for you and always treat you right. He sees you. He feels you. He lives for you. You picked the right one. Your heart knows all along.

Live every day in the presence of love and gratitude, and you'll see that life is just about that. You get what you give. No drama. Just love.

I hope these words of advice challenge you and make you think. However, in the end, you can take this letter, crumple it up, and throw it away, because everything explained here has already been done. You did it. You did it without a rulebook. You did it on your own and you survived. You moved mountains and you were great at it. You let love conquer you. You loved in return. You grew up. You are compassionate, strong as hell, vulnerable, open-minded, and capable of being in touch with your inner voice. Your soul is pristine and at peace. You know you are special, unique, and meant to be great. And you will be. Give it time and work hard. You'll figure it out. Best of all, you'll be okay because your number one fans will always be there for you, and it's okay to lean on them once in a while. Don't pretend to be an idea of someone else. Just be your true, authentic self, and you'll see how life will surprise you. Go out there and breathe.

Zania, count on me for anything. I will always be with you, protecting you.

Xoxo,

You, at the sweet age of thirty.

ZANIA SALA is a bilingual voiceover artist and singer. Juggling life as a mom, wife, and woman in business. Loving every moment!

2

Motherhood Happiness

MANUELA FRENCIA
Thirty, Italian

When I was twenty, I used to say that life would go downhill after twenty-five (how pretentious of me!). I look back at the past decade and it's like a blur of college parties, job hunting, dating, moving countless times, and at the end, trying to find my place in this world. As I think about it, my twenties were very stressful, leaving childhood behind and becoming a grown-up.

As I approached the dreaded thirties, I panicked a little bit. I was married with a small baby and had the body that went with it, not the sexy celebrity post-partum look. I wasn't the glamorous woman I thought I would be, but I was more than that. I was a mother.

What is thirty for me? Thirty is dirty diapers and burping cloths, waking up in the middle of the night to check if my boy is okay, and cooking three different lunches a day to see which one will be successfully eaten. Thirty is Friday nights spent eating pizza and watching a series on the DVR, breastfeeding sessions, swimming lessons, and play dates.

I traded my Prada purse for a Chicco diaper bag, high heels for sneakers, and lab coat for yoga pants, but I wouldn't change a thing. The real changes were not the material things, but inside of me. Something clicked, and I was in my place. I was no longer trying to fit in. I found the zone I had long been searching for.

Now that I am a proud, wise woman of thirty, I am poised to enjoy life as it comes. I live and breathe every new day as if it is the last. With children, time flies and they grow up so fast. Every day they learn something new, and they teach me how to be surprised at small things and to find the positive side to everything.

Motherhood and my new decade have given me a sense of place, of happiness—yes, that's what my thirties have been so far: happy.

MANUELA FRENCIA is an Italian living in the Dominican Republic. Single mom of a son. Juggling work with co-parenting. Many things have changed in the years since she wrote this essay, except for one: motherhood is still the most wonderful thing that could have ever happened to her, and her son is still, and always will be, her priority.

3
— *Today* —

MARÍA DELGADO
Thirty, Peruvian

Today I am thirty, and this is what I know:

-Love and compassion breed peace, healthier relationships, and a better connection with the world.

-Awareness is true consciousness. Get to know yourself and you'll get to know the world.

-You are not your mind or your emotions—you are the observer of everything.

-Don't judge or criticize yourself, others, or life. Observe yourself when you do—it usually means something about you.

-You are the painter of your reality: observe how your mind is conditioned to see the world, then patiently and lovingly teach it something new.

-Accept everything first. Acceptance brings change.

-Heal yourself. Go to therapy, spiritual retreats, and other places of self-nourishment. Take responsibility for yourself and your growth.

-Exercise and be as healthy as possible—it makes you feel good.

-Whatever you love to do, do it. Life gives back when you are doing what you were born to do.

-Whatever you choose to do, make sure it is for the good of others, too.

-Fear is blinding. Every time you feel fear, do something silly or tell the fear that you have things to do.

-Detach from your own story and open up to new perspectives.

-Be in the flow of life, as it comes. That is true happiness.

-You are a human with emotions. Be okay with that.

-Forgive your past or it will consume your present.

-You are perfect just as you are right now. Love yourself unconditionally.

-Don't compare yourself with others. Everyone has a journey. Live your own.

-Always be yourself. You were made uniquely to be just as you are. Being true to your heart is the best guide to good decisions. Listen to yourself.

-Learn to live in the unknown. Sometimes it's time to just be.

-God, Light, Your Center, the Universe, whatever language you speak, is ever-present. Let go and let yourself be guided.

-You are important because you are here. Everything else is an extra you give back to the world.

-Be kind. Be love. Be you.

MARÍA DELGADO is a Peruvian living in Miami. Imperfectly human. A music creator, business owner, woman, wife, and mother. Writing, whether on her walls at home, a napkin at a bar, a notebook, or her iPhone, has been her biggest form of expression and passion since she was twelve. She is growing, evolving, getting closer every day to the most authentic version of herself.

4

- The Eternal Transition -

JT GAUTREAU
Thirty-four, Dominican

"WE ARE PRISONERS IN THE PRESENT, LOCKED IN ETERNAL
TRANSITION BETWEEN OUR PAST AND OUR FUTURE."
Neil deGrasse Tyson

Before I introduce myself, I wanted to quote Dr. Neil deGrasse Tyson, the American as-trophysicist, because it's incredibly relevant to my life but also relevant to yours. Yes, you, reading this right now. You, no longer in your twenties but not yet in your forties.

My name is JT, and I'm a thirty-four-year-old singer-songwriter from the sunny and beautiful Dominican Republic. I currently live in Vienna, Austria, where the never-ending supply of schnitzels, wursts, and beer is a constant threat to my weight, especially now that I'm in my thirties. But I didn't start off as a singer-songwriter, even though I've been playing instruments since I was a child. Like many children from third world countries, you must study business, law, medicine, or engineering, otherwise you are boycotting your future. But we'll get to that soon.

I had a wonderful childhood filled with love, attention, the occasional smack in the ass by my mother, and lots of toys. I was raised as an only child, you see (own horn tooting alert!), a normal, non-spoiled one, I'd like to believe. My mother is a surgeon, my father a psychology major/marketing master, and both of them are also politicians. I know, I ask myself the same question: How did I end up as a singer, in Vienna? As a teenager, I was always playing music, writing lyrics, humming songs, drawing marker tattoos all over my body, and vicariously living through my favorite band's music videos, yet I never really thought about dedicating my life to music, not in the real world at least. Even though in my imagination I was a rock star.

After school I went to university and majored in marketing. And that was it. Adulthood had begun and my dreams got locked in a closet somewhere near my guitar. I graduated with honors and flew to Spain to complete a master's degree in advertising. My mom was proud. But while in Spain, I started playing guitar again and recording some music, and it became very clear to me what I wanted to do with my life. I called my mother and told her I was going to finish the master's program, but I was going to play music and write songs for a living. As you might expect, a huge argument followed, which led to her breaking off communication for some days, but I was determined! (She later understood and ever since has been my number one supporter.) I then completed a graduate degree in audio production and a postgraduate degree in audio engineering in Barcelona.

I recorded my first album in 2012, titled "Hay Veces." It was a compilation of songs in Spanish and it was a fantastic experience. Seeing my work and concept materialize in the form of a CD was something else. In 2013, I married a beautiful Polish girl and we moved to Vienna because of a job opportunity, and in 2014 I recorded my first album with all songs in English, titled "Crossing." I have been gigging all over the place since.

Now that I've told you a bit about my story, I'd like to talk to you about growth, the past, the present, and the future. For a while I was haunted by regret. I regretted not devoting myself one hundred percent to music earlier on, I regretted the years I invested acquiring various degrees in business that I was not making any use of, I even regretted not putting my wishes and desires ahead of anything or anyone else. But as Dr. deGrasse Tyson says, I'm in the transition between my past and my future. I've learned to let go of regret and realize that the only thing you can change is the present, and every day you should work toward the things that make you happy, even if you have to do some things that you don't like. Eventually, as time moves on, you'll be left with the good memories and the joyous moments. Plus, I wouldn't be where I am or think the way I think if it weren't for everything that I did and did not do. I learned this a long time ago, but only in my thirties have I achieved enough maturity to understand it and embrace it.

JT GAUTREAU is a Dominican-born singer-songwriter now living in London. His music is hugely inspired by pop melodies and hooks, modern beats and Latin-Caribbean vibes, and his style and sound can be described as unique, complex, dark, and high energy.

5

— What List? —

MICHELLE FAIRWEATHER
Thirty, Australian

Something happened to me during my twenty-ninth year. I started to feel old. Maybe it was when I saw the increasing number of gray hairs in the rearview mirror each morning. Maybe it was when I was tagged in a photo that was clearly taken to show my ever-deepening wrinkles. It may have been that Sunday when I realized it was taking me a whole weekend to recuperate after a not-so-heavy Friday night. Or maybe it was when I realized that certain body parts, which normally enjoyed a rather northern vantage point, had started migrating south. It could have been when I stopped going to weddings and started attending baby showers and, ever-increasing in popularity, divorce parties. It might even have been when my sixteen-year-old godson, the godson whose nappies I remember changing, called me for relationship advice.

Now I remember. The sinking feeling that life was well on the downslide to aging occurred when a good friend pointed out that my days of being a twenty-something female were numbered. I won't lie: Turning thirty sounded horrendous. I put on a brave face and told everyone it wasn't that bad, but really my trained-counselor self was only easing others' fears, because deep down I was dreading it.

Why was turning thirty such a dreadful experience? It was because something or someone somewhere was making me take stock of my thirty years and measure them against a list of expected accomplishments. I don't know how this list exists—it's not written down anywhere, no one tells you about it, no one hands you a secret envelope that self-destructs after reading, and it doesn't arrive in the mail disguised as a birthday card. However, the list is very real, and it appears to be available in any language. It exists inside every twenty-nine-year-old and is screaming out with every dwindling twenty-ninth year sunset.

It's the list that determines how successful you are. It determines how proud you can be at your high school reunions. And it gives you a method for measuring the productivity of the past thirty years. If you score well, you can kick back and hold your head high as you blow out those thirty candles. If you score badly, you'd better huff those candles out before you set the place on fire with the knowledge that you've got your work cut out for you before you reach the next milestone.

So what did I find when I sat down with pen and paper and the list? Under housing, I didn't have a picket fence and I was still house-sharing. Under relationships, I noted I wasn't married, and I certainly didn't have children. Under professional experience, I had yet to work in my field of study. And under assets, even if I counted my pushbike, I was pretty much asset-less. So which section of this mysterious list could I check off? I've traveled. I've traveled a lot.

I uprooted my life at twenty-seven and lived in three different countries. I've seen the gorillas in the mist in the depths of the Congolese jungle. I've watched the fireworks over Paris as the clock struck midnight on New Year's Eve. I've eaten a champagne breakfast in the Masai Mara and I've laid in between two sleeping tigers in a canyon in Bangkok. I've stood over the grave of the mighty King Henry, and I've learned what a joy blackcurrant and true Irish Guinness are. I've also clocked up enough frequent flyer miles to do it all again. Yet, when compared to the list, I am left with one measly section marked off.

Who is it that determines what the list should include to make a successful thirty-year-old? When compared to a mother or a wife on maternity leave from her dream job, why should I hang my head in shame and feel the need to explain being out of the country for three years? Why did I feel the need to uproot my life again at thirty and head home to my country of origin, in search of ways to mark more items off the list? What I should have done is asked my thirty-plus housemates to help me look for the originator of the list. That way we could have sent them a lovely gift basket, full of food that they might choke on.

My advice to all those twenty-nine-year-olds? If the positive in your life outweighs the negative, hold your head high and scream from the rooftops that you embraced the wisdom that being thirty brings. When that doesn't take away the dread, just remember a celebrity like Jennifer Aniston. At thirty she was still not married, not yet divorced, was childless, and had a dreadful haircut. Success is what you make of it. Ignore the list at all costs!

MICHELLE FAIRWEATHER was born in Adelaide, South Australia to British parents, and grew up with the aim to one day travel the world. While rapidly approaching thirty and after exploring the track far less trodden in places such as Africa and Asia, Michelle settled in the UK for three years. However, when the need to buy furniture and fancy cutlery became too strong, she returned to her hometown to determine whether it was still home. A graduate of psychology, Michelle knows this move will not be easy, but is excited about what lies ahead on the other side of thirty.

Problems You Don't Have

JOLINE MATIKA-RATY
Thirty-two, Canadian

A wise gal pal of mine once said to me:

Tanya: Did you get eyelash extensions?
Joline: Yes, and I hate them.
Tanya: Why?
Joline: Because they are uncomfortable and when they fall out, they take one of my
real eyelashes with them.
Tanya: Joline, stop creating problems you don't have.

Tanya's right. My eyelashes are fine just the way they are. Why did I get extensions? I didn't want to wear makeup on vacation but still wanted my eyelashes to look long and luscious. So it was somewhat logical. Right. Eyelash extensions, really? If ten-year-old me was told one day women would be gluing false eyelashes to their real eyelashes, I would have laughed and laughed. "Uh-huh, next you'll be telling me that in the future people will drink water out of bottles that they purchase at a grocery store." Exactly.

Anyway, back to the lashes. We women are bombarded with these types of "problems" at every corner. "You're too fat, you're too skinny, your hair isn't shiny enough, your teeth aren't white enough, your lips are too thin, you need shellac, your shoes are so last season, you are a size five, you are a size ten, you look good… for your age." We're told 3,000 times a day that we have 3,000 problems. It's almost impossible for us to stop creating problems we don't have.

I have taken Tanya's advice and applied it to many more aspects of my life. Now that I am in my thirties, I don't create problems I don't have, because there are enough real problems in the world. They deserve more attention than all the superficial problems directed at women who are beautiful just the way they are.

Now that I am in my thirties, I am happy with me, just the way I am. Don't get me wrong, I am no granola sister. I continue to have fun with beauty and fashion, but on my own terms. I put aside feelings of competition with other women, and instead celebrate their beauty and accomplishments. No more eyelash extensions, ever again.

JOLINE MATIKA-RATY is a tree hugger, animal lover, and mama of little maniacs.

– Living –

LAURA BARBOZA
Thirty-one, Costa Rican

At the tender age of twenty-eight, a wise gentleman in his thirties, named Mr. Oliver, said to me, "Your twenties are for learning and your thirties are for living." Those words landed with a heavy impact. I was learning a lot at that time in my life, but I was also eager to get past the uncomfortable Saturn Return phase I was in. Having just moved from Miami to Seattle, I was struggling to find emotional balance, professional prosperity, and growth amidst a new culture. In a broken economy, with a new set of acquaintances, I was unemployed, confused, and homesick. Reaching my thirties carried the significance of stability for me, especially after Mr. Oliver's words circled in my mind daily, and I was anxious to get there. I embraced learning my lessons, but I was just ready to live!

To cope with the changes, I turned to yoga and successfully reached an internal depth and awareness that I never expected to achieve so suddenly. Spiritually, I began to reach toward a higher self, while attempting to get through the inevitable daily challenge of emotional and mental transience. My ultimate goal was to reach my thirtieth year as a strong, successful, and serene being. I collected every bit of energy in me to make it happen. I was determined to shine, and not concede to the downhill effect most fear when reaching thirty. Supporting my idea of glowing rather than graying, I was informed of the concept of one's golden birthday, when the day of your birth aligns with your age, and magical moments arise. To my fortune and surprise, I was born on June 30th.

While looking forward to heeding Mr. Oliver's advice to live during my thirties, I set a defined two-year plan. I sought to complete a master's degree and expand my yoga practice to promote the goal of being in the best physical shape of my life. I also wanted to implement and practice grace in everything I did, said, and thought. Grace meant stability in many ways: handling anything that life blew my way with objectivity, managing confrontations and negative moments with ease, and becoming a centered person in every sense.

I've since come to understand that finding grace is a lifelong endeavor. Though I try, it's not a daily occurrence. This aspiration is still my ultimate goal, and when I stumble more days than I'd like to admit, I strive to be gentle and forgiving. Otherwise I remain humble and grounded, which is what matters.

I'm thirty, still learning, and proud to say I'm humbled every day. Learning and living are not mutually exclusive. They coexist the same way we do with individuals, emotional situations, and environmental factors. Where I find myself at thirty is not where society wants me to be or what pride led me toward. I've learned we don't have to fit in, or be comfortable, or make money to be happy. And isn't that the true definition of living?

LAURA BARBOZA is a customer experience research strategist living and learning in Seattle, WA.

8

Third Floor, Please

MARGIE SIMO
Thirty-one, Dominican

When I was twenty-seven, I told myself that if at thirty my life had not taken the expected course of marriage, children, and a nice house with pets included, I would make a radical change… and boy did I! I resigned from my job, sold my only material property, and left my country, my family, and my friends. With very few certainties and all my savings, I moved to New York and started a new life. That deadly combination of "I'm thirty and don't know what to do" prompted me to make a seriously risky decision. I still don't know whether it was courage or insanity. Changing my entire world led me to the least traveled road: the road to myself. The number represented a time of change, and though it was hard at times, the rewards have been incalculable.

Today I am thirty-one, saying with absolute conviction that I've never lived more intensely than I have this past year. I have dared to do things I never thought of before. I have experienced the full autonomy and freedom of decision. My biggest accomplishment is learning to cultivate feelings about myself, despite everything. The bad days continue, but the good days outweigh them. I see things more clearly now. There are things I don't do anymore. Some things I care less about, while others concern me more, but I'm learning to cope. Some desires go unfulfilled, and I have new fears and ghosts lurking, but inexplicably, I also feel a strange sense of "everything will be fine." I'm convinced this sense of belonging comes from myself and the maturity I've achieved.

I can't recall experiencing any of this in my twenties. I know myself better, body and soul, and that power is only mine. The invitation for my milestone party said: "Share in my arrival to the third floor!" I have arrived on a new stage, in a decade that is waiting for me to enjoy it. I will take the good with the bad, the crises and different phases—gaining and losing weight, wrinkles and gray hair, old and new relationships. I will receive the tears and laughter, the professional challenges, and the potential for motherhood. I will take all the surprises and disappointments, accomplishments and unfulfilled dreams. I'm eager to live my thirties like this. I'm confident I will stay intact in my essence, but different, by the end of it ready for the fourth floor. I can't even imagine!

MARGIE SIMO is a Dominican sustainable development professional and animal lover. She likes writing, prefers the ocean to the mountains, has a sarcastic sense of humor, secretly wishes to play the sax, and is tremendously blessed to have family, friends, and a husband that support her in all her craziness.

9

Ready for Life

CARLA WYSS PONCE
Twenty-nine, Peruvian

In less than three months, I will be thirty, and I am already window shopping for the dress I will wear at my birthday bash. I might be fifteen years older, but I feel like I am prepping for my quinceañera. I have to celebrate life, love, accomplishments, and most important of all, health. I have had some crises, but it's all part of getting older. I just hope I won't hear anything like what someone asked me in a hair salon once: "Do you want to try our new Botox products?" Good thing I don't need it. That's the spirit!

I look back and can't believe all I have done. I can't complain, I had a beautiful childhood, an unforgettable teenage life in Lima, an awesome time in college in the US. I had great experiences in my short, yet impressive career, and now I am enjoying married life in a beautiful place in Europe. I have enjoyed every single stage of my life and have to thank God for all the blessings. Cheers to that!

When I was a young teen, I dreamed of having babies at twenty-two, because I wanted to be a young mom. But at twenty-two, I was still in college, single, and partying in South Beach, but also dreaming about my Prince Charming. He would be tall and blonde, with green eyes, perfect hands, and a beautiful neck. He would be gentle, lovely, and romantic. I had to kiss a lot of frogs first, but incredibly enough, I just described my husband, Sam. And my prince treats me just like a princess! I learned from those broken hearts to appreciate who I have next to me. Now I wake up every day, open my eyes, and see the most beautiful and pure eyes I have ever seen in my life. That's what I call love.

Life has gone by quickly, and I don't know what else destiny will bring. I moved from Lima to Miami, escaped to London for three months and New York for six months, then went back to Miami, and now I live in Switzerland. Will I live in Japan, South Africa, or Australia next? Who can say? I know I need to enjoy today like there is no tomorrow.

I don't regret any important decisions I had to make in the past, because I believe that things happen for a reason. I follow my dreams, because I came to the conclusion that being successful is not about how much money I have, but about looking back on all my accomplishments, and the fight and work it took to achieve them.

I believe that you are the owner of your happiness. It is up to you to follow a path, even though there will always be obstacles. You need to learn how to overcome those barriers. Persistence is the key, and you have to keep dreaming. Inevitably, you have to live, experience, learn and fall. Then you stand up and do it all again. Sometimes justice is not fair, but believing the inevitable will help you be stronger, and allow you to keep following your goals. Life is not perfect.

I can have this and that, but still I want something else—it's just part of being human, I guess. But today, I am happy for all the good things, and thankful for all the bad things that taught me something. I am ready to turn thirty and ready for what the future will bring. I want more challenges and lessons along the way. Bring it on, baby!

CARLA WYSS PONCE is a professional communicator with great motivation and full of aspirations. Positive, dynamic, reliable. In search of creating memories and unforgettable moments with her family and friends.

10

Crossing the Bridge

VANESA PAREDES
Thirty-four, Argentine

I am an Argentine film director and producer, born in Buenos Aires, a city I describe as full of art and movement. My mother, a housewife with a taste for theater, drawing, and music, was the one who introduced my siblings (dancers, actors, and musicians) and me to the world of art.

I have always wanted to tell stories. When I was a young girl, I drew on every blank piece of paper I could find, invented and wrote stories, drew cartoons. With the help of my high school art teacher, I found the perfect profession: filmmaking. I started my studies at the prestigious University of Buenos Aires. Before graduating, I worked as a camera operator and video editor, first at a record company in the visual area, and later as an editor at an important company in the city.

Growing up in Buenos Aires, I was friends with children whose parents had come from Asia and many other countries in Latin America. I always had a special interest in the experiences of travelers and empathy toward immigrants. I wondered how it felt to live between two worlds. What was it about living away from your culture and your language? How did it feel to share and learn new customs and ways of life? I saw the pain of uprooting and the feeling of being between two cultures, without feeling 100 percent part of either of them. I graduated as an audiovisual designer, and in 2012, I made a lively short on this topic.

My life was good. At twenty-nine, I got engaged to my boyfriend of three years, a great man who loved me enormously. However, deep inside, I knew I was not ready to take that important step.

I had always been a curious person with an adventurous spirit. I felt that something was missing from my life. I felt the need to travel, to see the world, to explore, to hear stories, to be by myself. My family is very traditional. When I was about thirty years old, everyone thought it was the ideal time to get married and have children. I had found a wonderful man: Why shouldn't I marry him? I tried to commit myself to my decision to get married, because he was supposed to be the right one. But I was lying to myself and he sensed my doubts. He knew me well enough to see that I wasn't sure about it, so he asked me what I really wanted, and in that moment, I realized that I wanted to follow my dreams of traveling and exploring the world. We cried and hugged. We said goodbye and I made the conscious decision to change my life. It wasn't easy—I loved him—but it wasn't my time to be a wife and mother, and for him that was a priority.

After a few months, I got a working holiday visa in New Zealand and my adventure started. I was so excited and happy! I wanted to learn English, and I wanted to see the world. I couldn't believe that my life had changed so much in such a short time. I have been to twelve countries in the last three years. I have seen wonderful things, I have met many people, and I have had the opportunity to work on what I love. At the moment, I am thirty-four, and all these experiences have made me stronger and more independent. My life is a continuous adventure. I do not regret my decision. When you listen to your heart, there is no way things can go wrong. My ex-fiancé got married and became the father of a beautiful daughter. He is happy with his new family—I am happy for him and he is happy for me. We both fulfilled our dreams and we are still friends.

After two and a half years doing all kinds of work, but always looking for the opportunity to do what I loved, I found a way to keep working as a filmmaker in New Zealand. I have participated in various audiovisual projects and was presented with the possibility of participating in Crossing The Bridge, a creative collective founded by Mauritian anthropologist Sophie-Claire Violette and supported by creative editor Lucy Holland—and now, also supported by me as a filmmaker. We create visual and experiential projects with a strong anthropological focus. Our first project, *Crossing The Bridge: Exploring Identity and Belonging in Ashburton's Migrant Community*, told the stories of twenty-one migrants and their experiences integrating into the rural town of Ashburton, New Zealand. This project is extremely close to my heart as I can feel in my own flesh what my immigrant friends felt while living in Argentina.

With perseverance and following our hearts and true dreams, we can fulfill everything. Our work in Crossing The Bridge is the best example.

VANESA PAREDES is an Argentine producer and director. She believes in the importance of the plurality of looks in audiovisual media.

11

No Answers

YARIMAR URIBE ARIZA
Thirty, Dominican

I have recently been blessed with reaching thirty years of my life, and everything is supposed to be different, or feel different, or so people say. It doesn't. I still feel like a teenager when I see a guy I like. I still smile like an idiot when he looks my way or after he kisses me. I still do stupid things I regret immediately. I am supposed to be all grown up, yet I still feel like a kid.

I have gotten this far and don't have the answers. I have lived so much, but don't know where to go or how to get there. Things have changed, but I can't say how or when.

We are supposed to walk our paths and learn so many valuable lessons along the way, but I feel like I haven't learned anything, and life is ahead of me, waiting. Maybe it's not about figuring it all out. Maybe it's just about walking ahead and trying to be smart enough not to make the same mistakes. And, if by chance we are not smart and mess up even more, then maybe it's about having the strength to say: "I made a mess. Now let me try to fix it. And if I can't, let me move on and keep walking." Maybe it's not about "growing up," but about "growing wise." (I prefer the latter.)

I don't have the answers, but maybe... just maybe, I am not meant to.

YARIMAR URIBE ARIZA is just herself. A dreamer, a believer, a hopeless romantic, a writer of things the soul cannot say.

12

Anonymous Truths and Insights

AS TOLD TO LAURA SGROI

What you want at twenty-eight is not what you want at thirty-eight.

The secret is to find someone who loves you how you love to be loved.

I have dated boys and I have dated girls. I can't even remember some of their names. Then I found the male reflection of me. He made me feel alive again.

I found someone to love. Someone to give all my love to. He was taken, though. I wanted to prove to myself that I could go after him. I had never been bad before.

Sometimes I just want to run away and never look back.

I didn't grow up with my dad. Actually, I never met him. That is maybe one of the reasons why I was the girl who wanted to love. The one who would spy on lovers on the street. The one who couldn't sleep, wondering who would give her her first kiss but wouldn't play *La Botellita* (spin the bottle). I wanted to wait for The One. I would dream of walking down the aisle, hanging on the arm of the groom with the blurred face. Thank God for teenage years. Looking for love, full of hope. Feeling its presence all around. How can you be so sure about something you have never experienced? How do you know it's going to feel good? Somehow I just knew it. Songs, poems, and soap operas must be right.

People act like the land where they are from, barren or fertile.

Fear controls all our actions.

This child won't change me.

I evade responsibility and run away from my household routine in the name of travel for work.

I knew I would either leave him that day or stay with him forever.

My ovaries failed in my twenties.

I "accepted" his alcoholism because he was my best friend and I knew I couldn't have kids anyway.

My wife has always been a full-time student. It's time for her to work.

The trick is to have an argument without fighting.

We have no communities, so we want everything from our partners.

We must evolve, we must transcend.

She had plastic boobs. It was kind of fun.

Don't cheat. It's never worth it.

It took me a long time to feel like myself after giving birth.

He gets to have hobbies. I only get to work.

I can't believe this happened to me: I terminated a pregnancy.

Guys are intimidated by my professional success.

Some days I am a single mom, and when he is back, he treats me like a nanny and a maid. Still, I'd rather be a single mom than married with no kids.

I don't want to marry you and I don't want to have your kids. I am bored to death. And I'd rather be worried than bored.

Don't be stupid, don't look at his phone. The time that you waste looking at his phone could be used to work on your relationship.

Viagra killed him.

He said he loved me, but I couldn't have a child for him so he left.

His cheating hurt, but what hurt the most was when he said that he didn't love me anymore.

I am not afraid of him anymore. I am not afraid of leaving, of being without him.

He never complimented me. He never made me feel pretty. By the time he tried it was too late.

We grew apart.

I regret having my child.

I am clean and sober now and I need someone who supports my growth.

I thought I couldn't divorce. Don't let the stigma of divorce scare you. The law protects you.

Find a good woman to be the mother of your kids.

People say breastfeeding takes so long. Are you in a hurry to do something more important?

My family withdrew from me because of religion.

I worked really hard, and I felt taken for granted at home by my wife.

The real post-partum challenge is staying married.

I have been nurturing my marriage for twenty-five years.

You don't want to be alone at forty-seven.

A divorce will hurt as much as the process of fixing your marriage. So fix it.

I am just a hopeless romantic man.

She is so complicated.

ANONYMOUS Men and women who couldn't write their own stories, but trusted this book to share them.

13

God Prepares Us

SABRINA MÉNDEZ
Twenty-nine, Dominican

At about twenty years old, I heard that a woman's best age is in her thirties. I immediately thought, "By that time, most women have too many responsibilities to enjoy anything, and they're already getting OLD." Making all sorts of big decisions, I thought I was finally a mature adult enjoying life in my early twenties.

My younger years were full of good things that contributed to the person I am today. I have nurtured a lot of meaningful relationships, especially with my best friends and sisters, despite the physical distance that separates most of us. It seems like we have never been apart. My husband is the love of my life, my soul mate, and the father of my son. God's creation, my son is a perfect blend of my eyes and sense of humor and my husband's body and kindness. He is the reason we want to become better people every day, and the only one who makes me understand and love my mother more. But my relationship with Jesus was the most important one that I built during those years. Getting to know Him, instead of just knowing about Him, opened my eyes to a new purpose and dedication that will never end.

Now, at twenty-nine years old, I clearly see that my thirties will be the point of youth to experience new things while approaching them with a mature perspective. I will look at life with a newfound sense of gratitude. I will know exactly what I need from others and what I have to offer them. I will write, with my husband, our family's story and help mold our son's character.

Turning thirty is a lot to process, but I'm excited, feeling the best is yet to come. I am blessed to have meaningful people in my life and the ability to enjoy them. With great anticipation and hopefulness, I trust that God is preparing bountiful blessings.

SABRINA MÉNDEZ is an island girl living in North Carolina. Never misses a chance to travel, eat well, or enjoy good wine.

14

Overcoming Abuse

JOHANA HERRERA
Thirty-three, Nicaraguan

I started changing after I had my child in my twenties. I fought all the time with my partner, who was a drinker. Then when I got mad, I abused my child. It was almost a daily routine. I was working, but I had no peace. The money my partner made was only for him. I met friends to grab a drink or party. I was not paying attention to my child, and I didn't care what my mother said. I felt miserable and worthless. When my partner said he was leaving, I would beg him not to. I was down on my knees asking him not to leave, and he would push me away. I was always going after him. I didn't care about my child, only him. He manipulated me, saying, "Who will want you with a child? You are fat, ugly." But as time passed, I changed. I have worth, more than him. And I said, "If you want to leave, just go. I don't care."

At twenty-four, I almost lost my child. The government was going to take him away from me. I used to hit him and tell him that I didn't love him. Then my boss told me I was worth a lot and I would overcome this. "You have to change, you don't have to take all that, someone who abuses you." My partner and I split up for a while, but then he said he was going to change. We got back together, but after a while everything started up again. At that point we had two children, and I was thirty.

He started seeing other women and I was tired. I told him I didn't love him anymore. There was no communication, so I realized that staying together because of the children was no excuse. I felt horrible. I cried. I had no pleasure from sex. I didn't feel anything. He would get mad when I told him he bothered me.

He started a relationship with another woman, but she cheated and left him. His family didn't want anything to do with him, so last year he came back to me asking for another chance, and I said, "No, no more chances."

My oldest son used to say, "Poor dad," so I took him back again. He always came home late, and during the months that I was not working, I asked him for money to buy food, and he said that I asked too much. I told him "You are in my house and you have to help. We have bills to pay. If you are not going to help, then get out." He said I had changed a lot and I told him he made me change.

Now it is different. I love my children. My son sees it, and says that I don't yell at him. Now his father pays rent, buys his food separately, and lives in my house like a tenant.

Now my oldest son is thirteen years old and the other one is eight years old. They are my blessing. They help me at home. My partner comes and goes. I pay a girl to babysit my little boy. She drops him off at school. My oldest son goes straight home after school, does his homework, and makes dinner so it is ready when I get home.

JOHANA HERRERA is a mother of two boys, big heart in a small body. Still discovering herself.

– Incomplete Equation –

CARLA SANTANA
Thirty, Dominican

For as long as I can remember, I had this moment of my life coldly calculated into this perfect mathematical equation:

18 (Age when I graduate from high school) + 3.5 (College years) + 1-2 (Years for a master's degree) + x (Marriage) + y (Children) = <30 years (An accomplished and happy life!)

Three years ago, I realized that this calculation had some factors in reverse order, which was not bothersome as it does not alter the final product, but others simply were not in the equation.

Two years ago, I discovered that I would not be the one to solve the formula. If it is true that in my hands I was living the process, it is also true that I wouldn't find the solution.

I would be a spectator of the solution just like the figures in it.

Today I received, with deep gratitude, the third decade of my life. To my surprise, it is much better than what I designed in my mind back then, my mathematical equation. Like purchasing an airline ticket for the Dominican Republic (my home country) but ending up in China (an exciting unknown destination), my thirties are totally different from what I expected, but they are an adventure that promises to be much more fascinating than I could have planned.

I thank my parents, sisters, nephews, uncles, cousins, friends and all those complicit in this adventure of mine, according to His will and purpose. I thank God, as the author and finisher of my days, my best formula, for the plans of welfare and not calamity, and the fulfillment of His word. Thank God that today I understand my equation was shorter, but unlimited.

Thanks for giving me more than I could think to ask for. Welcome, my thirties!

CARLA SANTANA is a woman of faith, and an unconditional daughter, sister, aunt, and friend. Moon, scenic skies, coffee, and gourmet cooking lover, always smiling, grateful for life.

Stigma

RACHEL EVERITT
Twenty-nine, British

How could getting older not be a good thing?

At sixteen I left school, got my first full-time job, and got engaged—it was all just so brilliant. I bought my first house at nineteen, got a good-paying job I wanted, and was married by twenty-one. Getting older had been nothing but kind to me—I was in control of my life, living as an adult, and content with where I thought my life was going.

I thought that getting older was something that was measured by what you achieve, so I never actually gave aging a second thought. Then everything changed. Getting older became something to dread. I got divorced at twenty-four, my decision. The woman I had become was a far cry from the girl I once was in high school, when the relationship started. It was a good time to start over before children made an appearance, and I had only myself to look after.

After a few months of adjusting to being single, living alone for the first time, paying bills independently, and living it up with my friends, I realized all the years and achievements I measured life by had been deleted, and ultimately replaced with a feeling of failure. I was divorced, living alone, and struggling to pay my mortgage. The only thing I had going for me was my job, which I appreciated, sometimes.

Talking to friends one day about meeting someone new, I came up with a boyfriend checklist. The list itself isn't important, but I was adamant about one thing: not dating a guy over thirty. I was only twenty-four, so this seemed reasonable, right? Wrong. I could not have been more convinced that thirty was just too old. I didn't want to date someone who had reached thirty and not settled down, thinking surely something was wrong with him. It was narrow-minded and naïve, but it was how I felt.

I got into a relationship that lasted nearly four years. Those years were full of more achievements, a measure of how well my life was going: nice holidays, a new dog, a new job, and a new house. Then it ended, not by my choice this time. Once again, I felt like all my achievements had been deleted from the record, aside from my job. Except, this time I was twenty-eight and heartbroken.

Getting older was suddenly the last thing I wanted. It had been nearly ten years since I'd left home, but all I wanted was to go back and have my Mum take care of me. This wasn't even an option as I worked far away and needed to be near my job. After all, it was the one constant, aside from family and friends.

So here I am, trying to let go of the stigma I attached to turning thirty and the conviction that life is measured by achievements. I am not pining for things I don't have, or wishing the things I have were different. The only measure I want in my life is that I am alive and living. I don't believe things happen because of the age we are, but because of who we are. I hope that by my thirtieth birthday, I won't feel old, even though I still think thirty is old. At least I'm only going to be thirty, and not forty!

RACHEL EVERITT is perhaps the clumsiest person you will ever meet. Who knows where her life is going, but she believes that one day she will be perfectly content, no matter who or what is involved. Loves a laugh and tries not to take anything too seriously, although she has the bad habit of being "the sensible one," which at least saves her from too many embarrassing photos and memories.

17

Happy Medium

MASIEL PORBEN
Thirty-one, Dominican

My thirtieth birthday arrived four months before our wedding day. Since we were spending most of the time finalizing details of the wedding and arranging the honeymoon, I didn't have time to organize a big birthday celebration. Dinner and dancing with close friends at a venue with an outdoor terrace was the winning plan. The next day I treated myself to a nice facial and massage. In hindsight, booking those treatments the morning after the celebration was not a good idea. At thirty my body simply doesn't handle alcohol in the same way. When the therapist saw me sitting quietly on the couch drinking water, she must have known. She said, "Don't worry. I'm going to make that hangover disappear." I guess that was my first lesson as a thirty-year-old: Alcohol is not my friend anymore. And the second lesson was even clearer, to look after my skin.

Turning thirty did not cause an existential crisis or major life reassessment for me. At younger ages, I never had a clear idea of what I wanted to achieve by the time I hit thirty, so when the time came, there were no leftover checklist items to stress about. Traveling and living abroad were always on the agenda, so I moved to Europe at twenty-three and stayed. The freedom, the food, the people—it all still amazes me after eight years.

Finding love had no deadline, either. My outlook toward marriage was defined by the mantra, "Better to be single at twenty-five than divorced at thirty-five." When I was planning our wedding, there were lots of articles in magazines and blogs about the benefits of marrying after thirty, or the joys of finding your partner early and marrying young. I never found an article that discussed marrying exactly at thirty, like I was. Maybe there's something to be said about the happy medium.

It simply didn't bother me to turn thirty last year, perhaps because I was in a truly happy place. I was about to marry a wonderful man whose love made me realize that all those stories about soul mates are true. I liked my job, and by having a demanding role, I felt challenged and engaged. And lastly, I was in good health, something easily taken for granted. Turning thirty brought a bit more confidence and self-assurance. The twenties are about friends, parties, insecurities, studying, all non-stop. In my thirties, life feels a bit more relaxed—at least until children enter the picture.

108

MASIEL PORBEN was born in Santo Domingo, where she earned her bachelor's degree in economics. After living in London for twelve years, she now lives in Chicago with her husband, Paul, whom she married the year she turned thirty, and their daughter, Victoria. Masiel works as a finance trader, enjoys baking, and thinks yoga is the best exercise for body and soul.

- Life Is Good -

SUSIE DANTZIG
Thirty-one, American

As a child, thirty was old. Even when I got to college, I thought my twenty-two-year-old RA was old, so thirty was ancient. A thirty-year-old was a grown-up, someone with a nice-paying job, a house, and kids, a person who others called "sir" or "ma'am."

Now that I am thirty, I don't feel the need to adhere to any pre-conceived notion of what I thought thirty should be.

I have been in a loving, committed relationship for almost five years. We live together, work together, play together, and have committed ourselves to each other in every way, but we feel absolutely no need to get married, let alone have kids, anytime soon. We enjoy having the time and financial freedom to go out to eat where we want, travel, train for races, play in the local orchestra, and live in the city. The kids will come in another five years or so, and we'll enjoy each other in the meantime.

I went to a top-ranked university and at times I feel like I haven't been as successful as my colleagues. But, while those goals are worthy to strive for, I have accomplished so much outside of the office. I ran three marathons, traveled the world, and earned a master's degree. I play in the community orchestra, and I'm writing a book to teach children the violin. It may be a while before I rise above middle management at the office, but I love my job, and I make a salary that allows me to take care of myself and enjoy the activities I love.

I don't mind that thirty is not what I imagined, because I love where life has taken me. Who knows where I'll be at forty, but if I am as happy as I am today, life will be good.

SUSIE DANTZIG grew up in the D.C. area, earned a B.A. in music and biology from the University of Virginia, and furthered her music education with a master's in music business from the University of Miami. She currently resides in LA, where she works for a movie studio.

The Thirties Came in Spain

GODE SEGURA AMARANTE†
Thirty-one, Dominican

It is complicated to be part of a culture in which most women think being complete means being married with kids, but even so, my experience has been different. I'm very proud of what I've achieved in my professional and personal life. I'm grateful for my family, especially my parents, because without them I would not be the person I am today.

Everything started in 2003 when I was almost twenty-two years old. I always loved the idea of living in a different country on my own, one of my main objectives being independence. While preparing to take the English test for my application to the University of Miami, since I was almost done with accounting school, a friend started talking to me about Europe, specifically Spain. I thought: "Okay, let's see what Spain has to offer." I applied to several master's programs that I liked, some with the same English test as UM. I was finally admitted to a school in Madrid.

Madrid has taught me the most important things in life. I am stronger than I thought, alone in a different culture, far away from those I love the most. Spain has given me great friends, great loves, and amazing moments as a student, traveler, and human being. I worked hard, and am lucky to be where I call home today. At twenty-five I worked for a multinational firm in Barcelona in foreign projects. I became a Finance Director for a US subsidiary in Spain at twenty-nine. Today, at almost thirty-two, I am Head of Finance of three more subsidiaries.

Thank God for technology keeping my relationships with family and friends just as close as they were on the day I moved away. In essence, our souls and minds are together forever. But I miss having someone to share my life with. In Madrid, I've experienced something I will never understand, something that happens to my successful female friends too. It seems my success makes men afraid of me. The macho mentality puts us at a superior level, which these men are beneath, and according to them, we will end up leaving. Most of them don't realize that what matters most is what is inside us.

Not everyone is meant to end up in a couple. That will come for me if God decides it's meant to be. In the meantime, I build and maintain my own sense of happiness by living as if it's the last day of my life. Over time, I have become more demanding and picky in my thirties, because I realized I am a treasure.

Age is deep inside, thirty is just a number, but what matters is the knowledge we gain through time and what we give to others.

GODE SEGURA AMARANTE† was born and raised in the Dominican Republic, later based in Spain. Finance director experienced in auditing, internal control, and finance management. Enjoyed traveling, writing, singing, and dancing. Characterized as being a hard worker and a friendly woman. Success was her main objective.

Real Life Begins

YAHAIRA SOSA MACHADO
Thirty-two, Dominican

I am thirty-two and expecting my first child. When the thirties were approaching, I was torn between economic independence, the power to control my time, and the pressures of being successful. I come from a developing country, with longstanding traditions and underdeveloped views on sexism, and with little hope of improving in the near future. I grew up thinking that a defective woman is one who hasn't gotten married and had children long before her thirties.

I reached a good position professionally, I am well-paid, and have flexible hours. Arriving at thirty with no husband and no children was only a half success. All my friends had families already, and I was alone on my island, always looking for younger acquaintances to share in my singleness. I felt I was the only single lady turning thirty on the face of the earth.

At twenty-eight I met my current husband, who was only a couple years older, yet had already been married and had two children. We got engaged the day I turned thirty. Those were the circumstances of how it all happened, but today I understand it is the right age to make that kind of commitment. I had the opportunity to study everything I wanted, to work at what I love, and visit many other countries, for work and pleasure. I reached my desired position at work and enjoyed the economic independence it brought, the car and the apartment I wanted.

I have felt the maturity of choosing a companion for the right reasons—not because he was the "best match," the most handsome, the richest, or the most popular—but because he is a responsible parent with a steady job, and he is mature enough to sustain a healthy relationship with his first wife, besides being a family guy.

YAHAIRA SOSA MACHADO is Rodrigo's mommy, second mom of Oscar and Paula, companion of Máximo. A public servant who works so that her daughter has the same opportunities as her sons. Faithful believer in God and his presence in her life. Daughter, friend, sister.

To the Maximum

SONIA YOUNG YIM
Thirty-four, American

"THE ONLY TIME YOU REALLY LIVE FULLY IS FROM THIRTY TO SIXTY.
THE YOUNG ARE SLAVES TO DREAMS; THE OLD SERVANTS OF REGRETS.
ONLY THE MIDDLE-AGED HAVE ALL THEIR FIVE SENSES
IN THE KEEPING OF THEIR WITS."

Hervey Allen

Things that get better with age:

    wine

    cheese

    art

    designer handbags

How about biological age?

Benefits:

    higher self-respect

    wisdom

    greater sense of well-being (*cough* money *cough*)

    naturally better at things with more experience (sex, anyone?)

Drawbacks:

    wrinkles

    don't lose weight as easily

    keep forgetting (what was I saying?)

    suddenly, reading small print becomes a challenge

So, what does it mean to be in your thirties? What I really think—it doesn't freakin' matter.

But this is what aging has taught me:

    In anything, there's always a good side and a not-so-good side.

    You can never bring back your past, no matter how much you dwell on it.

    You can't reverse anything that already happened to you.

    If you can't be happy today, you certainly won't be happy in the future.

So, let's celebrate our thirties to the maximum. Shall we?

SONIA YOUNG YIM is a wannabe creator who is still finding her voice. A used-to-be rebellious employee who is all about non-conformity. And an advocate of simplicity who is yearning for happiness, fulfillment, and freedom.

22

It Will All Work Out

MARILU CRISTINA FLORES
Thirty-one, American

In my twenties I accomplished numerous things: I was married, moved away from my home permanently (or so I thought), and was pursuing the career I had always dreamed of. I gained recognition professionally, traveled to many places I had longed to visit, and had a lovely home in Southern California.

Five years into my first marriage, we called it quits and just a short time later I found myself engaged to someone else. We married a year into dating.

As I approached my thirties, I found I was no longer in love with the career I thought I always wanted and it felt like the few choices I did make for me were not heavily appreciated or accepted by my partner. I chose to go back to school and pursue marine science and took a position in marine conservation, which paid me a third of what I'd previously made, even as a young professional in high school!

While I was happy professionally, working outdoors in the sea and teaching children about the importance of conservation, I quickly found myself stuck in an unhappy marriage with a spouse who was less than there and in-laws who could fill the pages of horror novels.

When my ex-husband left me, just two weeks after my thirtieth birthday, I wasn't devastated, but relieved to be free of his wandering ways and exhausting family.

The day after he uttered the word "divorce," I hopped on a plane and spent a month visiting friends in Vermont and New York. When I returned to Miami, I packed up my things and relocated to Vermont. Just like that. It was the freest I had ever felt up until that point in my life. I had no plan and minimal savings, but somehow I truly knew it would all just work out. I'm sure to many it seemed odd, unexpected, and completely out of left field! But somehow I knew this was what I had to do.

Now if you know me, you know I am #TropicalLife for life, so this was a huge change for me. Before my life in Vermont I was convinced anything under 75 degrees was freezing and ungodly.

While I didn't know it yet, in Vermont I would experience the worst winter there since 1859, and I would find myself moving into an area completely new to me: digital marketing.

It was during my time at Keurig that I really began to realize what diverse work experience I had and how I truly was capable of anything I wanted to accomplish.

I met someone, a man, through a friend and for the first time in my life I took my time:

took my time to decide.

Not just about who I wanted to spend my time with, but to truly decide what I wanted to make of my time, my energy and of the things I was so extremely passionate about.

In May of 2015, in the winter that felt like an eternity, I had a rather crazy dream about putting on an #EcoFashionShow, and that next morning I reached out to the people who were in my dream, who—crazily enough—had recently started a nonprofit and had been discussing a fashion show for months! But they had no clue where to start, and so began this new chapter in my life.

I started organizing the show, making phone calls and emailing people I had met throughout the years.

Everyone I reached out to said, "YES! We'll help you!" They donated goods, time, the venue, everything! It was crazy!

Everything was happening just like in my dream. I decided to relocate back to Miami in August of 2015, my new love in tow! And work continued on the fashion show. I also became involved in other projects, such as helping Surfrider, a nonprofit I had been involved with in California and for a few years in Miami before I left for Vermont. Shortly after my return I was asked to become a board member—one of my lifelong dreams!

Finally, the day of the fashion show arrived and within an hour we were completely sold out, raising well over our expectations and generating interest for another show and other events.

From this began an overnight business, as people wanted to hire me for my new-found digital marketing and social media experience.

I turned thirty-one on August 23rd, and upon reflection on my birthday I realized how much more I know now (clichéd, I know), and despite what many would consider some epic failures (two divorces and a fifteen-year career I left), I learned that without those marriages I would have never been able to appreciate the man I am with now, who was willing to leave all he knew behind and relocate to Miami with me because he believed in me and my dream, who wanted to see me grow professionally and personally. And without my previous career, I would have never learned what I now know, which has helped me immensely as a social media specialist.

At thirty-one, I am living the life many strive for over a lifetime. I love what I do! I have accomplished work-life balance and every day is a new, welcome challenge.

I have gained financial freedom I never thought possible and have learned to nurture a healthy, mature relationship with an age-appropriate man who appreciates me as much for my flaws as for my accomplishments.

I can't wait to see what this decade has in store. There will be ups and there will be downs I am sure, but the wisdom gained from my experiences in my early twenties will surely see me through them.

MARILU CRISTINA FLORES is a digital media producer, marine conservationist, and Florida Regional Coordinator at The Surfrider Foundation.

23

Hey There, Sexy Mama

VERONICA BARRIOS-GARCIA
Thirty-eight, American

Dear Self,

You think you are pretty awesome, right? You are twenty-eight years old and you look amazing. You think you are fat, but I wish I looked like you. Your future is bright, after finishing college and beginning your career. Life is ambitious—weekdays and debauched weekends. You've had your share of late nights, spontaneous trips, and reckless decisions. Your thoughtless risks are incomparable to the obstacles ahead. Your biggest responsibility is paying the rent, and your monthly budget is forty percent nightlife and alcohol. I miss you!

You've made some admirable decisions. College degree: awesome, that's helped you a lot. Husband: good choice, he's a keeper.

I know you are in your honeymoon, lovey-dovey phase, but your husband is truly amazing. In ten years you won't want to jump his bones as often, but you will always be happy he's by your side. You are a better woman with him and you guessed it, he's still around and going strong. Just please make sure he gets into the habit of trimming those nose hairs: It's a real turn off.

You think you've experienced stress in college and your career, but it's a cakewalk. Wait until you experience your first anxiety attack, which naively you'll mistake for heart failure, asthma, or diabetes. You will have gray hair, but only a small patch, a la Rogue from the X-Men.

Good news: That mysterious single thread of hair you periodically find on your neck only when it's grown three inches is gone. Bad news: It now shows up on your boob. (Sorry.) However, your body is still a fearless vessel full of energy and longevity, and capable of great endurance, even though these days you'd rather take a nap than do anything too physical. Don't be too disappointed, it's only because you're busy working and caring for your family. Yup! You're someone's mom! Scary, I know, but surprisingly you're pretty good at it. You've never been very maternal, but trust me: You will be a good mother—maybe not a model parent—but loving and very patient.

Motherhood has brought you great happiness in your thirties, and although you still struggle with the transition, it has been a blessing. I'm sure you are curious about work since career is your biggest priority these days. Work was and still is a great part of your life, however, balancing it with your family has been a challenge. Your professional choices have brought you great joy, you've had the opportunity to contribute to many amazing projects and some not-so-amazing ones. Your greatest accomplishments, though, come from the choices you've made in your personal life.

I hope this letter serves as a guide as you enter your thirties and gives you a bit of perspective about the choices ahead of you. Continue to follow your heart, stay close to family and friends, because they will last, and don't lose your sense of humor—it's your best attribute.

By the way, you are pregnant! So lay off the *vino*, you sexy vixen! Oh, and one last thing, dye your hair black. It really brings out the green in your eyes.

Best,

Your Future Thirty-Eight-Year-Old Self

Despite failing miserably at her childhood dreams of becoming Miss America or the next Madonna, **VERONICA BARRIOS-GARCIA** continues to impress as a storyteller, creative television and event producer, community activist, mommy, and lover of all things funny. Born in New York City and the child of Argentine immigrants, Veronica attributes her always-optimistic disposition to her mother, who encouraged her to see the good in all people and situations. She is married and the proud mother of two rambunctious boys. She resides in Miami.

24

Living from the Heart

LIBBY CREAGH
Thirty-three, American

I never lived a conventional life, and turning thirty was no different. Some women feel pressure to conform to societal expectations as they reach this fulcrum. I saw thirty as a time to decide what I wanted out of life, and to act on it. No more waiting for my life to find me. It was time to walk the walk, using my actions, not my words.

I spent my twenties working with nonprofits to affect social change. With strong ideas about the way the world ought to be, I thought I could bring change through protesting, canvassing, and lobbying elected officials. I was sure that by compiling enough facts and communicating with the public, people would see reason and act in their own best interests. Some positive change happened during those years, on a national level and in smaller statewide and neighborhood campaigns. Just as many decisions went in the opposite direction, though, and I began to see it was all part of a cycle.

In my late twenties, I wanted to shift careers. I still believed in activism, but my personal focus changed from affecting the outer world to helping people access a more profound change within. I turned my yoga practice into a career, getting certified to teach and diving into a lifetime of training. I wanted to learn more about sharing the "yoke" of yoga, on and off the mat.

The year I turned thirty, I was unemployed and in-between careers. After spending months searching for traditional work, I cobbled together opportunities that added up to exactly what I needed to make ends meet. For the first time, I realized that income didn't need to be tied to a traditional forty-hour-per-week job. It was also the beginning of living with trust that the universe would provide what I needed.

I was immersed in a world of spirit, practicing and teaching yoga, loving my work, and expanding my worldview. Shortly after taking the leap as a yoga teacher, I was given an opportunity to practice and teach in Central America. That's been my life path ever since—traveling and learning about yoga, culture, and the human spirit, while living fully and authentically from the heart.

I'm thirty-four now. I never had this much trust in my twenties—I'm grateful for the lessons I learned then, which allow me to live my dream in a gypsy lifestyle now. The advice I would give my thirty-year-old self is: "Worry less and trust more."

LIBBY CREAGH is an E-RYT 500 yoga teacher who has been sharing and practicing yoga, meditation, and reiki for more than twenty years. Now based in Tampa, FL, Libby leads retreats and yoga teacher trainings every year. Find out more at www.essentialyouyoga.com.

- No Regrets -

JOHANNA SALAZAR
Thirty-three, Colombian

At twenty-nine, I felt it was the end of my youth.

Boy, was I wrong. The moment I turned thirty, twelve months later, I actually felt younger than ever. I can't tell you what happened or how, just that it did.

Today, my priorities are different. My family has always been very important to me, but now they feel more valuable to me than ever before. Now, I cherish and work on my relationship with my mother every day. I am more grateful for everyone in my life and for the opportunities that come my way.

At thirty, I began seeing life in a different way, with more powerful youthfulness and fearlessness. What matters most to me now is living happily, with no regrets. Knowing that I pursued all my goals and dreams and lived my best life is the most important thing. I'm more aware of the girl I was, the woman I am, and the person I want to be. Thoughts of starting a family began circling in my head as well, strange as it was, since I had made my career the priority for so long. Now I live in gratitude every day.

Relationships are different. In my twenties I was not very aware of what I was building. Now, I feel blessed by my decisions and the relationships I have built. Good and lasting relationships have made my personal and business lives so much better.

I am happy, grateful, passionate, powerful, and fulfilled. I live every day with purpose. I recognize that my passion for the cause is bigger than my ego. Core values drive the achievement of my vision. I am a fearless, determined, and persevering woman. Every year I feel younger and stronger. If this is what it feels like to be thirty-three, I can't wait to be forty-three.

JOHANNA SALAZAR is a media disrupter. Content/media/digital strategist. Professional change-maker, future author. Enjoys laughing at her own jokes!

My Girls Have What I Didn't

ANGÉLICA GUEVARA

Thirty, Nicaraguan

When my thirties approached, I said, "Thirty is just another year." Then I realized that three decades means I'm getting older. It's time to grow up and mature.

The center of my life is my girls. I have to fight for them. I have to gain respect, because I want them to have a good example from their mother. I think we women have to value ourselves, because if we don't, nobody will.

I used to think that without my husband, I was nothing, but that changed when I turned thirty, partly due to my job. I always had part-time jobs so I could spend more time at home. When my husband arrived, the food was ready, and his bed was ready so he could rest. Now I have a serious job and I contribute, which demands respect in my home.

I have good memories of my mother, but not my absent father. He abandoned my mom, so she was mother and father at the same time. I want my girls to learn that we don't have to be with a man. We can do it all by ourselves.

Mom and I went through a lot. My mother taught me good manners, principles, and how to respect others. I didn't see fights, and I learned how to be responsible. We were nine siblings! I didn't have the chance to go to school, but I learned how to read and write. I want my girls to have what I couldn't have. That's my challenge. When my husband lost his job, my daughter was in first grade, and it was an issue. We didn't have money for registration and school supply kits, but it didn't matter; she had to go to school. It is sad not to study and I made sure they would have what I didn't. I say to my big girl, "You have to value everything, especially school."

I met my husband when I was fifteen and he was seventeen. I got pregnant when I was sixteen and had my first child at seventeen. We moved in together and we fought so much. He was not working and we went through very hard times. We were the same for a long time, but then we started to change. Since then, we have had a very good relationship and good communication. We talk with our eyes. If we don't like something, we say it. The most important thing is communication.

I am proud of myself. I am a fulfilled woman. And thirty is the best age ever.

ANGÉLICA GUEVARA is a mom of three, married to her childhood sweetheart, would do anything for them.

Not an Inch Different

PATRICIA CARABALLO
Thirty, Dominican

Today dawned and I'm not even an inch different. And yet today is an important day, because I celebrate my thirtieth birthday.

I'm happy.

Though there are stigmas that come with this decade, I still feel young, with a long way to go.

When I was a little girl, I thought that by thirty I would have accomplished many things: the perfect job, the perfect husband, the perfect children, etc. I did not complete the list, but I am very proud to have achieved so many other things that I never imagined I could do, and most important, I have come to understand that perfection is not always the right thing.

I'm not married, but I am accompanied by someone who helps me grow every day, has taught me what it means to love, has taken me to see the world on unforgettable trips, and who simply makes me very happy.

I have no children, but I smile at the thought that, in the future, I can enjoy their antics and will be ready to accompany them throughout life, teaching them the values that my parents instilled in me.

I do not have the perfect job, but I have a job that challenges me, which has allowed me to prove that I am an experienced professional and youth is not an impediment to excelling in an area where the gray hairs usually win.

Thank God for the many opportunities. Thanks to my family and friends who go along with me on this journey, and thanks to life itself. Today I am a woman full of joy, celebrating my thirties with new goals and dreams!

PATRICIA CARABALLO is an economist of the world, New Yorker at heart, and Laura Sgroi's first friend ever (they met in preschool when they were three years old).

Walking in the Right Direction

GLADYBELL BRUNO
Thirty, Dominican

I can say that my thirties have been such a blessing. When I was little, I used to think that at this point, all aspects of my life would be resolved, but the movie is still not even halfway over. The journey has been beautiful thus far, with its fights—some of which I have won, and others that I've lost—each leaving, in a very particular way, a mark and a lesson.

At this age, we put emotions aside to be more analytical, more deliberate, and more objective. We start looking at life from a different perspective, even those things that seem to be so complicated. The fears and uncertainties about the future start disappearing. We feel more control over our lives and acquire maturity. We are more thoughtful before making decisions, because we are not thinking only about ourselves anymore, but about our environment and the impact these decisions could have on our loved ones. We start loving our people more, enjoying those family moments, which we used to see as obstacles to going out with friends. Instead, we take advantage of every opportunity, outing, and reunion to spend quality time in harmony with our family at home… our sweet home.

We learn to be by ourselves and enjoy it, because the everyday worries keep us so busy that in a quiet moment of rest, we see an opportunity to embrace the company of a good book or nice music, to escape from the chaos and routine for a little bit. We create stronger bonds in our friendships. We remember with laughter and nostalgia the days of adventure when nothing mattered, or when going out, meeting new people, flirting with boys, and looking cute was all that mattered. We strive for learning and gaining skills that add value to our lives and are compatible with our goals. We stop wasting our time trying things that will not contribute to our careers.

Is it age? Or the fluctuating economy? We become more stable at work, even enjoying it and missing it. We become more disciplined with our finances, budgeting for future plans and brainstorming projects that would produce economic growth, while keeping a close eye on money management.

We start taking care of the planet, using organic products, eating healthier, working out, and routinely visiting the doctor. We also start doing good for society, because we understand the need to give back to the world.

In our thirties, we finally learn that happiness is a journey, not a destination. Then we start enjoying and delighting ourselves with the small things in life. The most beautiful thing is to find the purpose for which we were created, a purpose we can only discover by accepting Jesus as our Lord and Savior, and then we start walking in the right direction.

There is nothing like being thirty, and I am happy with this beautiful age.

GLADYBELL BRUNO is an entrepreneur, co-founder and commercial manager of Yrka S.R.L. Marketer by profession and passionate about cosmetics and health.

29

Then and Now

XOCHILT BAZÁN
Thirty-three, Nicaraguan

At thirty, I had many follies in my life. The worst was sleeping with a married man, solely out of lust. As a result, I had a baby. I gained a son, but it was a mistake to get pregnant from a one-time fling. When I realized I was pregnant, it was a big letdown. I always thought that I was going to have only four children. I was not planning to have more. This would be my fifth child.

When he found out I was pregnant, he wanted to start a family with me, so I decided to join him, even though I didn't love him. I told myself that it was time to settle down, because the fathers of my other four kids never showed as much interest as he was showing. I decided for my baby to build a home with him. Days before we moved in together, he backed out. It was a big disappointment for me, because he got back together with his fifty-five-year-old wife and left my child on the side. I had always dreamed of getting married, of walking down the aisle wearing white, and I thought this was the moment, but it didn't work out. I decided that I would never again be with other man.

In my thirties, I have matured a little bit when it comes to my relationships with my children. Before, I didn't pay much attention to them; other things were more important. After thirty, I wanted to become a better mom, more devoted. I prayed to God to teach me how to be a mom first, above all other things. I never had a good relationship with my parents, but now at thirty-three, I have a good relationship with my mom and a super relationship with my kids. Communication with my children has improved a lot. I talk about my previous life with my daughters so they don't make the same mistakes, so they see that they can be different.

I got married. I regret it because I had the same illusion that it was going to be a different life. He was younger and a very jealous man. I started seeing life differently. Before, I didn't care about anything. Everything was debauchery. I wasted money. I liked to go dancing. I never had vices, but I loved to dance. If someone invited me, I'd ask anybody to watch my kids and just go. But with him I learned to see the value of life, despite the life that we were living together.

Now I have matured as a woman. If I seek another partner someday, I won't let love guide me. I'll follow my own intelligence. I've never dated an older man, but now I would like someone who knows what he wants.

I have also matured when it comes to money. I think before I buy. I still have debts, but I value money more. I have more children, but I manage my money better. Before I was a little vain, caring more about what we would wear, not checking if we had any food at home. Now food is first, and then everything else.

I realize that I depend on a higher being. I grew up in a Christian home and used to go to church, but I never recognized who God was for me. Now I ask Him to be in charge of everything that I do, because I have given my life to Him. Good or bad, things happen for a reason. The best thing that ever happened to me was maturing spiritually. If I give my life to God, if I ask Him for help, my life will be different, because I depend on Him. With Him, I'm on the right path. My children were rebelling at one point, because of what they learned from me. Now that I recognize Jesus as my savior, they have changed. I see the difference in them.

Thank God I haven't had any health problems, except for some minor issues with my lungs from smoking at my job in the cigar industry. For years I never smoked, but when I got pregnant with my last child, I would smoke a little bit now and then, and after I gave birth, I started smoking frequently. I know I shouldn't do it, because it will make me sick. I do eat less now, while I ate like a pig before. I didn't care how I looked, but now I care more about myself.

Thank God I have arrived where I deserve to be. No matter how messy my life was before, I have always been a good worker. I am where I am today because I have done a good job. I deserve it and I'm worth it.

After I hit thirty, I got interested in studying, in the intellectual life. I am very interested in my English classes, and next year I'll study information technology. A desire to improve myself has taken hold, and I'm asking God for help so I don't slow down or stop. Before, I used to start things and not finish them. Now I need to finish what I start.

I talk to my children more. I used to make up stories, any excuse to go out. I was afraid of what people would say, but now I'm more honest. I feel confident as a person, as a woman. I feel complete in my thirties, no matter how much I have suffered. I feel proud of myself, because I am a single mother, even if I wasn't always an excellent one. I see that my kids have grown up. I was able to raise them, and that is beautiful.

XOCHILT BAZÁN, born in Honduras, lives in Nicaragua, single mother of five beautiful children, proud grandmother of two beautiful girls. *Tabaquera*. Blessed by God, in love with her family, her job, and her friends.

30

— Epiphany: Life Gets Better Every Year —

SONYA MOORE
Thirty-one, American

At twenty-six, I realized, "Every year, life gets better," my epiphany. Aside from a brief exception, this has been true for me since I was eighteen. I went through a temporary post-college, mind-numbing, low-paying, cold-calling sales job crisis, but survived. I realized that crises in life are easier to deal with if you look at them as scenes from a movie.

Another epiphany I had at some point while approaching the Thirty Year Milestone is that life rarely turns out according to plan. Yes, I know this is fairly common knowledge, but it took me a while to realize it myself.

Life loves to throw surprises at you, sometimes every now and then and sometimes with the incessant speed of an automated batting machine spitting out baseballs. Thanks to a few of those unexpected surprises, my life has turned out nothing like I planned, but instead, extraordinarily, incredibly, delightfully better. When I was little, my original plan was to get married at age twenty and have lots of babies right away so that I would be a young and cool mom. I could never make up my mind about what kind of career I wanted to pursue. I went through wildly diverse and consistently short-lived phases of author, pilot, interior designer, flight attendant, photographer, travel writer, and auditor, to name a few. I never had a clear vision of my professional future. But when I was nineteen, I went to Europe for the first time, backpacking through France for two weeks. After that, my life and dreams would never be the same.

The travel bug bit me, and it must have taken a seriously big bite, because it turned me into a hardcore addict. Ever since, if I don't leave the country at least once a year, I suffer. I love my country and I love coming home to it, but my soul isn't at peace unless I get to step on a plane and fly away every so often. During the remainder of my college years, even as a dirt poor student, I managed to finagle ways to leave the country every year: a semester studying abroad in the south of Spain, a one-month stint as an English teacher in a summer camp in Belgium, a two-month internship at the US Embassy in Guatemala. I also settled on a field of study during that time. Still mostly clueless as to what I wanted to do, the only thing I had figured out was that I wanted to get paid to travel, so I got a degree in international business. I studied hard, worked hard, and slept little, working three jobs and going to school full-time. It was stressful and exhausting, but it was a good time. College was fun and social, and classes got more interesting the closer we got to graduation.

I graduated and paid my dues for a couple years, with jobs that I either didn't like, paid just enough to cover my bills, or both. I couldn't imagine at that point that my professional life would ever get any better. But then, out of the blue, it did. When I was twenty-six, I got my first dream job, working as a regional account manager for an international marketing company. The job responsibilities required me to travel to the Caribbean every two weeks. I'll always remember the euphoria of receiving the job offer letter from that company and the excitement of my first trips to the islands.

Although that job didn't turn out to be utopia—along with the tropical travel came high stress and long work hours—it was still the coolest job I'd ever had, and I would have been content to stay there for five more years. But then, once again out of the blue, an even better opportunity fell into my lap. I got a phone call from a recruiter and he offered me a job to travel the globe, developing international business for a company in the hair care industry. This job isn't utopia either, but overall, I'm extraordinarily blessed to have it. I have a great boss, fun coworkers, wonderful clients, and I've gotten to see and experience many amazing places and things because of this job, from the Hagia Sophia in Istanbul to the breathtaking vistas of Machu Picchu to the spectacular views of Victoria Peak in Hong Kong. I've seen the beaches of Rio de Janeiro, the islands of Fiji, the vast diversity of Australia, the pristine elegance of Singapore, the sea breezes of Puerto Rico, and the gracious hospitality of Korea—and I've only had the job for four years.

Along the way, I've met many marvelous people and had countless unexpected adventures. I would say that I'm living my dream, except I never dreamed of anything as amazing as this. When I think about life as I know it now, at age thirty-one, and I think back to that dark, anxious time of twenty-five, I want to send consolation and hope to anyone who is going through a similar dark tunnel. There is light, joy, and happiness at the end of the tunnel. Life can and will get better; you just have to keep walking, and enjoy the journey.

SONYA MOORE loves people, language, connection, and making things happen. For the past two years she has been teaching yoga and consulting in Southeast Asia and is currently based in Siem Reap, Cambodia. Her favorite thing about travel and living abroad is connecting with people of different cultures and discovering the local cuisine, ambiance, architecture, countryside, music, customs, and unexpected adventures that await in every destination.

— *Calling Mom* —

SKY STERLING
Thirty-one, American

I was certain that on the day I turned thirty all of the questions I'd ever had in life would be answered. I'd open my eyes the morning of my birthday knowing exactly what I was supposed to do with my life, and more importantly, how to do it. Nope. Other than figuring out how to deal with the worst hangover I'd ever had, I was not any more insightful than the night before.

The one thing I realized the morning of December 24, 2011, is that it had been a full year since I had spoken to my mom. We'd had an argument on my birthday the year before, and I couldn't tell you what the fight was about because I don't remember. But being the headstrong women that we are, neither of us had reached out in over a year. A lot can happen in a year.

Leading up to my thirtieth birthday, I decided to completely change career paths and move to a new city, a difficult decision, but even more strenuous without the support of family members. And for me, family consists of my mom. My dad passed away when I was thirteen and the rest of my relatives live in the Dominican Republic.

I'm not sure if it was the milestone birthday that drove my mom to call me that morning, or if she just wanted to end the silence, but hearing her voice, along with the emotions of catching up on a year's worth of living, made me realize that the woman I'd argued with for years, the woman who I thought I had nothing in common with, is actually an older, wiser, more jaded version of me.

SKY STERLING was born and raised in the Washington Heights neighborhood of New York City, and she credits her writing style to the city's fast pace. Sky moved to Los Angeles to pursue a career in writing, and hopes she does not end up waiting tables.

What I Really Want

LAURA MICHELLE ABRÉU
Thirty, Dominican

Since I was little, I've always said that by this age I wanted to have a family and a good job. In the Dominican Republic, women are born to start a family. This is not a decision. It is instilled in young women since childhood. Now I am thirty, and I want the same cliché, but with a bit more bravado.

I am able and willing to continue growing professionally. I have a job that I like very much. Though I would like to earn a little more, I cannot complain. I want to own a business but still do not know what kind. I think over the next few years I will look for that opportunity.

Currently, my relationships are better than ever. During adolescence and college, I went from place to place, experiencing new things, choosing what to take and leave. I am the result of everything I took and left in those stages, and my relationships are as well. Today I have my true friends, my family, and my partner. The people I want around me pass on true love and positive energy to help me, and that teaches me to be better every day.

Spiritually, I have my own way of thinking. Never do to others what you would not like them to do to you. Do not hurt anyone. Be fair and positive. My relationship with God has greatly improved, but not as much as I would like. I've had painful experiences lately that without God and my loved ones would have been impossible to bear. I love God and Jesus more than anyone, but have always known I needed a congregation to learn more about Him. I have tried, but I am just too lazy to go. Thank God for a family and a partner who are taking me in the right direction, and I love it.

I am super quiet but adventurous. I crave learning new things, something that will never go away. My thirties are the time to make new plans and gain new experiences, or relive what I already know. I worry more and I am concerned now, because I want my own family to enjoy for a long time. Thank God I'm good in that respect, just waiting for the right time to start adding children, and with God's help that will be soon.

The thirties are for knowing what you want in your life and doing everything humanly possible to get it, because you know it will bring you happiness. Live the years fully, enjoy them as much as possible, and don't think about what you're missing, but what you really want.

LAURA MICHELLE ABRÉU puts God first. Caribbean woman. Loves her family! Miguel and Rafa's mom. Loves eating and traveling!

33

— Natural —

ANYA PIÑA
Thirty, Dominican

Turning thirty seemed to be more of a sin than the celebration of another year of life. Everybody was surprised: "You are turning thirty already? Uyyyy!"

For a moment I thought I had to pay a fee to this body for having survived so many years. I have never hidden my age and I would never do it now that I'm in my thirties. In contrast to many women, I feel very satisfied with everything I have achieved in these fifteen double springs. I feel more prepared, more beautiful, and more confident. I feel more interesting and mature, and others notice. And what I project seems to attract!

When entering your thirties, you hear a lot of advice: "You must watch your diet, exercise, apply anti-wrinkle cream, leave behind a few pieces of clothing," and so on. Then you begin to practice the ritual from beginning to end: covering yourself with cream every night, eating salads, not sunbathing, renewing your wardrobe, and joining the gym. You notice that you continue to act like you are twenty-eight and gradually give up the new rituals, because you're confident that you are still just as "divine" as five years ago. Error!

The true nature of the "thirties" is not at exactly thirty, but after thirty-five.

Enjoy your thirties, girls. They are wonderful!

ANYA PIÑA is a fashion writer and marketing telecommunications analyst. Lover of animals, pizza, and tattoos. Married to her soul mate and mom of two dogs.

Life Continues to Flow

PATY "MARIPOSA" HERNANDEZ
Thirty-four, American

My thirties have been the most challenging and also the most liberating. I celebrated my thirtieth birthday in a small community in El Salvador, surrounded by friends, while serving as a Peace Corps volunteer. We celebrated with food, laughter, and music—a lovely way to begin my thirties. After I left the Peace Corps, I moved to Las Cruces, New Mexico and began my dual masters in Public Health and Social Work. Originally from Miami, Florida, and raised by Cuban parents, I wanted to move out west and see what it was like to live close to the Mexican border. After living in El Salvador, and hearing so many tales from people who emigrated from there to the United States through Mexico, I was curious about border issues. During my time in Las Cruces, I broke out of my comfort zone and took the lead in numerous student organizations, work projects, and personal journeys. I developed leadership skills and surrounded myself with positive and upbeat people, characteristics I have embraced since the Peace Corps.

In May 2010, my life changed dramatically as my older sister, diagnosed with non-smoker's lung cancer, took a turn for the worse. I rushed home to Miami to hear that she only had a few weeks to live. I was distraught at first, and then became strong as I held her hand each day. I was the one who told her she was going to die. I worked with her to write her will, as no one else was able to do it. The night before she died, she awoke from her drug-induced haze and asked me for permission to leave. I granted it, and then informed my family it was time for us to say goodbye. I remained by her side until the caretakers took her away.

A year later, my mother was also diagnosed with non-smoker's lung cancer. I was in Nicaragua at the time, working with a non-profit organization for my public health internship. Again, I rushed home and remained by my mother's side for six months until she regained her strength. Once she was better and her cancer was in remission, I returned to Las Cruces to resume my studies. I graduated with a Masters in Public Health and a Masters in Social Work in May 2013.

I lost my sister in her physical form, but I know she remains by my side. Since she left, I have followed more of what my heart has told me and less of what was expected of me. I have recently moved to Nicaragua, where I work for the non-profit that gave me my internship. My outlook on life is optimistic. I always have a smile on my face and a giggle in my throat.

Recently I met the love of my life, a person who complements me in every way. I look forward to every day with a heart full of love, joy, and happiness. I feel stronger every day and am guided by a positive energy force called Ki. In April 2013, I also became a reiki master to assist people with healing energy, so they may continue to live their lives to the fullest. I am blessed with the gifts I have been given, and those I can share with others. I am blessed with family and friends who support me in all that I do, and love me just the way I am. I am thankful I can share this story with pride and happiness.

PATY "MARIPOSA" HERNANDEZ was born and raised in Miami by Cuban parents who were passionate about travel. As a toddler, Paty recalls traveling by boat, airplane, and car with her family. She has continued traveling around the US, Latin America, and Europe, seeking new adventures and sharing her healing gifts wherever she goes. Throughout her thirties, Paty experienced many life-changing moments such as the deaths of her older sister, mother, and partner, Joel. She also chose to walk the path as an entrepreneur and founded her own practice called Mariposas Holistic Healing.

35

Male Version 3.0

IGMAR URIBE
Thirty-one, Dominican

I was born in Santo Domingo, Dominican Republic, or as I like to call it, *"Plátano* City." My father, Servio Uribe, like every other father, is a superman; he is an actor/director/professor of theater, a poet, an artistic lighting specialist, a charmer, a nature lover, and well-rounded Dominican *tíguere.* My mother, Lidia Ariza, is an actress/director/professor of theater and a theater owner. My father prefers tragedy, while my mother favors comedy; this made a difference in my character.

I grew up in Gazcue, a quaint neighborhood in the center of Santo Domingo, playing in the gardens of the National Theater and stealthily breaking into the Palace of Fine Arts, where my father used to teach, to catch the latest play, watch the National Ballet rehearse, or simply wander around looking for something to grab my attention.

As a kid I was always anxious to be an adult. I wanted to be Porfirio Rubirosa! I used to daydream of how I wanted my life to be, and for quite a while it turned out pretty close, except for the Rubirosa flavor. Growing up I was convinced I wanted to work in a strictly corporate environment wearing a suit and tie, behind a desk, somehow exposed to different cultures, with a chance to travel the world.

Upon high school graduation my priority was getting a job and making money, so I hit up the newspaper classifieds and found a position that fit my skills at the time: speaking English and knowing how to use a computer. I called them and got an appointment for an interview. After the interview, the manager said, "Everything is fine, you are a good fit for the job, but you are only seventeen years old. So legally we cannot hire you." I was bummed out, but she continued, "As soon as you turn eighteen, if you still want the job, give me a call." Six months later I had the job.

At twenty I moved out of my parents' house, which is a very bold move in Dominican society. I was making my own money and I wanted to be fully independent. Then something unexpected happened. A childhood friend from school—a beautiful, enormously intelligent, very funny, kind-hearted girl who was way out of my league—looked at me as more than a friend. The universe conspired in a wonderful relationship. It flourished quickly and everything seemed to be simply amazing.

Three months into it, my company was relocating and offered me the chance to move with them, initially as a trial for three months. After discussing this with my better half, I was off to incredible India. Then the trial period came to an end and I was offered to stay permanently, and at that point the only thing I wanted in the Dominican Republic was my girl, but I had this great opportunity, which I did not want to lose. I had to have both! She accepted my daring proposition. We married and started a life together in a land far from home, having only each other. Years passed and we moved to a different country, traveled throughout the world and enjoyed life to the fullest. Sadly, six years later the relationship ended, but the strong friendship and unconditional love remain.

Now that I am in my thirties, I work in a corporate multicultural environment, but without the suit and tie. I have traveled the world, felt very loved, and experienced many of the things I daydreamed about as a kid. I can't complain.

Everything changes and so have I. I have become somewhat self-centered, because I don't want anyone to depend on me. Someone once said, "The truth is everyone is going to hurt you. You just have to find the ones worth suffering for." I, on the other hand, don't want to hurt anyone or be worth suffering for. Will I stay like this?

I see my life at this moment as a new chapter; I feel that little by little I am breaking away from a completely paved and structured life. I pay more attention to the things that matter. I am thankful. I tell people I love them. I take risks. I act foolish, not taking myself so seriously. I have as much fun as I can, all the time. I use every opportunity I can to make others feel good. The only thing I am certain of is that one day we will no longer be here. I don't want to uncover the mystery of why we are here or what my purpose is. I am just going to enjoy the heck out of it.

This is how I see my life. Balanced between happiness and sorrow, comedy and tragedy.

IGMAR URIBE was born in Santo Domingo, Dominican Republic and he is now a pseudo world citizen. Daydreamer, lover of arts and sports, but a non-practitioner of both. A simple, good-natured, down to earth kind of guy who enjoys life to the max and treasures family and friendship.

36

– In My Own Hands –

PATRICIA M. CEDEÑO DE LOS SANTOS
Thirty, Dominican

When I was in my teens, I never imagined that one day I would turn thirty. As a girl, I pictured a thirty-year-old as elderly. A teenage boy said to me recently, "You're thirty?! But you have no wrinkles and look at your body!" I just laughed.

Many things are not as I thought they would be. My responsibilities and commitments are bigger now, but an interesting stage in my life has begun. My sweet thirties are welcomed, with new opportunities for personal and professional development. I am a woman in the prime of my life, with achievements and many new plans on the agenda. I am more mature and able to make better decisions. This age is a rich blend of youth with more experience, and I love it.

The experiences I've accumulated over the years have made me the woman I am today. With a more defined personality, fewer restrictions and taboos, I feel freer, confident, more open.

Each stage of life has good things and not so good things, but the importance lies in living each stage to the fullest and taking advantage of the lessons it offers. My life has been a journey in which I laughed and cried, enjoyed and suffered. I've made mistakes, I've fallen and gotten back up, and I have positive memories from it all, because I really lived.

I probably still have more than thirty years left to live, and I don't know what's waiting ahead. I think this stage marks the rest of my life; what I do today will define its course, and I'm in my own hands.

In childhood and adolescence, parents make most decisions for you. Your twenties are more independent, but your parents are still standing by. Starting at thirty, even though your parents will never fail to be by your side, you run it all on your own. It is an age to make important choices, an age of challenges and—why not?—fun.

PATRICIA M. CEDEÑO DE LOS SANTOS is a civil engineer and classical ballerina, an art lover in all its expressions. Loves traveling and having new experiences. Enjoying time with family and friends is one of the most valuable things in her life, which is even better when it includes music and a glass of wine.

37

Attitude and Acceptance

KIMIKO HOSAKI
Thirty-one, Canadian

I spent most of my twenties:
- Rushing to grow up
- Awaiting the golden age of thirty, when everything would be clearer
- Dating the wrong guy, knowing all along
- Trying to make it work
- Trying to find the "love" I had before
- Working extremely hard on a career that I would later walk away from
- Stressing about the past and why bad things kept happening to my family and me
- Trying to find myself by packing a bag and traveling the world
- Trying to make myself feel beautiful with makeup and hundreds of hair colors
- Seeking acceptance from my friends

I learned at thirty:

-Things don't get clearer once you hit thirty, but you face decisions with a stronger sense of self and more knowledge and understanding to make the right decisions.

-It's okay when relationships don't work out. Accept when it's not meant to be, and don't waste your young years with someone who doesn't enrich your life. Don't settle.

-I never really knew what love was until the moment I found it.

-It's okay to change career paths, each one sets the building blocks for your next step.

-Don't stress about the past. Life has a funny way of showing you when you are headed down the wrong path. Let hard times teach you to build strength and face the world.

-Traveling in my mid-twenties was the best thing I did to find and accept myself.

-Exercise is a good habit, because makeup and hair color don't hide cellulite.

-You learn who your true friends are. If you feel like you have to work for acceptance, they aren't your friends.

The best lesson I have learned and live by every day is:

If you wake up day after day and don't feel happy about something in your life, whether it is a relationship, a job, or the place you live, change it. Everything will work out in the end if you face the world with a positive attitude and acceptance.

KIMIKO HOSAKI is the founder and strategic director of K.H & co. Her ambition, determination, customer service, and uncanny business savvy have resulted in an impressive catalog of achievements and a wealth of experience amassed over twenty years in the hospitality industry. Her aversion to being pigeonholed and desire to always think outside the box are what separates her from the masses. No task is impossible, no issue is too stressful, and no goal is unmanageable.

38

How My Mother Taught Me to Love

LIA SEIROTTI
Thirty-one, Venezuelan

Some people come into our lives and we feel instant chemistry. With little effort we form a friendship that is not easily broken. Others require time, and with great difficulty we work to build those relationships. Still, in the face of rejection, if we counter with love, we can create strong bonds. That is what my mother taught me.

My mother says I rejected her almost immediately when I was born. It could be because I was dealing with the pain and symptoms caused by a slight birth defect, but I suspect my real defect was being born with a tendency to be less affectionate than most humans. From then onward, I've continued being somewhat cold. To this day, I prefer not to have unsolicited skin contact, I rarely ask for hugs, and I am extremely uncomfortable when strangers touch me. I am perfectly content this way. Deep down, however, I know this personality trait has always bothered my mother. In fact, my mother might well be the exact opposite of me; she is more open about her emotions and is not afraid to let her feelings show. Perhaps these are the reasons we didn't have that instant chemistry the day we met. Rather, our bond is the product of a resilient effort made by my mother to win my affections over time.

It was with courage through the worst of times that she single-handedly built our relationship. When I was hospitalized at the age of two, my mother dropped everything in her life to advocate for me. With much hardship, she traveled great distances in a developing country in order for me to receive the best medical care. She stood up to doctors and demanded that I be treated the way she instinctively knew was best. Later, when I was eight and we were immigrants in this new country, I was hospitalized a second time. My mother spent every night at my bedside. She comforted me through the physical pain and the fear I felt. Despite the fact that I was not very communicative or affectionate, she stayed with me. Then, when I was diagnosed with a different disease at the age of twenty-one, she took care of me once again. My mother knew it was important for me as a newlywed to maintain some dignity. For almost a year, she came to my house weekly to inject my medications so that my husband wouldn't have to see me that way. When I soiled myself in my own bed, she cleaned me. When I lost more weight than I expected, she took my dresses in so that I didn't look as sick. And when suicidal thoughts left me debilitated, she cleaned my house and cooked for my husband.

Ten years have passed since my mother last took care of me, but when my older sister called me recently to tell me my mother was in the emergency room, I dropped everything. It was the middle of a workday. Hardly thinking and without packing any clothes, I shut my computer down, got in my car, and drove six hours to be by her side. To be honest, all those moments in my life when my mother had taken care of me didn't even cross my mind. I was driven by pure instinct. It was almost a sixth sense that I felt. I knew exactly what my mother needed, and I knew that I was the only one who understood the proper way to care for her. I knew she would need someone who could advocate for her, because that was what she did for me when I was two. I knew she would need someone who would stay by her side every sleepless night, because that was what she did for me when I was eight. And I knew she would want dignity and privacy because that was what she gave me when I was twenty-one.

Immediately upon arriving, I organized and cleaned her room, because that was what she meticulously did for me every week when I was sick. I asked her if she had eaten and taken her medication, even when I knew she hadn't. I knew I had to make small talk and pretend we weren't all scared. I knew it was my job to downplay the entire situation as if it were normal, because I have learned to never let the fear of chronic illness show in your demeanor as caregiver.

Now that my mother is recovering, we hardly speak of illness; she knows I'd rather not get emotional. But we both know now that I am capable of caring for her and that I will when she needs it again. In fact, I don't remember if I hugged her or kissed her, but I know I cared for her and loved her.

Doctors say there is a vital moment immediately after birth during which a mother and child should have uninterrupted skin-to-skin contact. They say this is key to any mother-child relationship. While that may be true, I have learned that if you missed that chance you can make up for it with resiliency, compassion, and consideration. Without realizing or intending to, my mother taught me so many invaluable lessons about love. She has shown me that even if you feel you already deserve it and shouldn't have to, you can work to earn someone's affections. She taught me how to nurse someone you love. She modeled what unconditional love looks like and taught me that it can triumph over unrequited love.

LIA SEIROTTI is an educator and writer who is passionate about telling stories. Through her writing, she inspires others to love themselves and find the courage and freedom to be authentic.

39

— Life, Love, and Me —

YOSELY CEDANO
Thirty-five, Dominican

It all started with the best birthday party I've ever had: An all-day celebration starting early at my office and continuing at the "must-go" bar of the moment, where the guy I liked used to work. It was a disco theme, with friends and family, dancing and drinks, my favorite cake, and a great atmosphere. No other birthday celebration has surpassed it. Not that they haven't been good or special, but the excitement I felt turning thirty was second to none. It would be a stage to face challenges that life had not given me the opportunity to take on in my twenties.

My first big challenge came only one month after my birthday. I suffered a medical malpractice that almost cost me my life. It made me stronger, thanks to God and my family, who gave me so much support. The experience taught me to appreciate things, feelings, and people around me, which did not matter before. It made me realize how much my family and friends love me. It taught me positive lessons and scarred me only with a thin line on my body, which I call my "lifeline."

After that, I started doing things that I always wanted to do but never got around to, like going on a cruise. I reunited with a group of friends on a cruise to the Caribbean Islands, one of the best vacations I've had in my life. I would do it again without thinking twice, not only for the sea, discovering new places, good company, and great food, but also for the joy of having a good time.

In matters of love, this phase marked a before and after. A short time later, the guy from the bar and I gave it a try. We had a normal courtship like any couple in Santo Domingo, with dates, nice treats, calls, and text messages. Then we got tired of that and decided to get married!

We gave ourselves three months to arrange everything, just in time for my birthday month, August. I did not want a classic wedding, just something simple. In those three months, the hustle was unparalleled, with apartment hunting and buying appliances, and what were we going to do on our wedding day?! The rings, the witnesses… I think about it now and it's still exhausting.

The court made a mistake when they wrote our date, and there was no space available on our planned date, so on the 19th, we had to change the wedding from August 20th to the 25th, meaning more time to stress out! The Big Day arrived, with all the rituals of hair and makeup and not enough time. It was a very emotional civil ceremony, intimate and familiar. Then we had lunch for the attendees. Everything went as we had planned it a thousand times.

Now that we are married, back to reality. The first months of marriage are very beautiful, because of the illusion and idealization of the other person, but at the same time it is very stressful to do your best at everything as a new wife: the house, food, clothing, and… that's right! I still have a job! When that stage is over, the stress decreases a little, and more of the day-to-day is enjoyable together.

After almost two years of marriage, we decided to relocate to another country, Mexico. I love to travel, but this was a big challenge because we were leaving behind many things and emotions: so much love, my dear family, my friends, my place, my memories, and my country. I felt I had left behind everything that once belonged to me. It's been a year since we came here and the change has been positive: better jobs, better quality of life, less stress, and no power blackouts like in Santo Domingo! Starting from scratch is always going to be difficult, but it provides the opportunity to correct mistakes, and that's the life lesson I took from this change.

The great challenge I face today is the most beautiful and happiest of all: motherhood. I am seven weeks pregnant, and it's been only ten days since I found out. We are happy and thankful to the Lord for this and many blessings in our life as a couple. From now on, I want to live every day of my pregnancy to the max, enjoying the whole process of awaiting the birth of my baby. Once my baby is born, I ask God to give us wisdom and strength to guide and help him or her to live a fulfilling life.*

*Sadly, after this was written, Yosely lost the baby and her next one. In March of 2016, she delivered a healthy baby girl and they named her Lía Isabela. God bless them!

YOSELY CEDANO is now back in her home country, the Dominican Republic, after years based in Mexico, She enjoys exploring places, people, cultures, music, and movies. A dreamer and at the same time a very realistic and practical woman.

40

Growing Pains

DR. DENEIA Y. FAIRWEATHER
Thirty-two , American

Turning thirty meant change:
  Arrogance to humility
  Living in black and white to living in gray
  Hiding from myself to facing myself
  Material growth to spiritual growth
  Living unconsciously to higher awareness

In my mid-twenties, I had it all figured out. I had a family and career as a teacher. I was well-traveled, with ambition and the will to succeed. I had triumphed over a lot and deserved all the good to come. I exercised frequently, and my health and my son's health were great. I had a house, a car, and all the material things that make an individual feel secure and successful.

I was accepted into a PhD program to be trained in my dream vocation as an applied anthropologist. At times, I was extremely self-righteous and arrogant. My attitude was nasty.

In my late twenties, I no longer wanted to be with my son's father, and moved out with my son. I was missing something in my life and felt bored being in a relationship. I was able to survive on my own, so I had little patience for others who made excuses for why they couldn't. I am appalled at my treatment of my son's father. He did everything he was supposed to do as a father and a man, and I was never satisfied. I do not wish to be with him, but I could have shown him more compassion.

In retrospect, I believed I deserved better and would quickly leave anyone behind who I thought was beneath me. I wasn't honest about my weaknesses, but would take any chance to flaunt my achievements.

At twenty-nine, life suddenly happened. In the course of three years, I was in a car accident, involved in some legal trouble, and my home was burglarized by a close friend. My income declined dramatically as my expenses increased. I began to feel sorry for myself and wallow in the pain, drinking alcohol daily.

Every day I had questions. Where did all of this come from? Why me? What did I do to deserve this? I thought I had done everything right.

I couldn't focus on my research. I grew anxious and spent the majority of my day worrying. My thoughts controlled everything. My thoughts were holding me still. It was a vicious cycle. I felt bad because I wasn't focusing on my son like I was supposed to. I broke up the family. I doubted my research and my capabilities. Then I would feel worse, realizing that I had these pitiful psychological problems, while others in the world had concrete problems.

How can I help others with my anthropology if I can't even help myself? Every day I thought like this, from the time I woke up to the time I went to sleep. It was exhausting and extremely unproductive.

Now, at thirty-two, I am slowly getting over myself and learning how to tame my mind. I have recognized some things about myself. In my twenties, I was deeply insecure, fearful, and angry about many things, so I responded to the world with arrogance. The arrogance hid what I was not willing to face.

I knew the first step I needed to take was to be honest about my weaknesses. I did not know it all. In fact, I knew nothing at all. My tone and body language needed improvement. So did my time and financial management. The advice I was so quick to offer former students is what I had to apply to myself. I needed to practice what I preached.

Next, I had to stop feeling guilty about breaking up the family. Western society does a great job of promoting the nuclear family as the foundation for a child's success. But my son, as a black male in the United States, could become just another statistic because he didn't have that family structure. It was a constant worry for me. I had to forgive myself and realize that individuals create their own reality, so it is okay.

Most important, I needed to develop genuine compassion. The only way I could begin was by harnessing self-compassion. I used to feel compassion while working with students and members in the community, so I made a vain attempt by offering time and money to causes. In retrospect, I did these things to make myself feel important, while showing others I was the best. I learned that compassion for others is not genuine without first having compassion for yourself. I could not offer the world what I was not able to offer myself.

If I want to contribute to this world through anthropology before I die, then I need to work on myself first. I need to keep promises to myself and, more important, forgive myself and keep moving forward. I thank the universe for presenting these challenges, because I need to grow.

Whenever I heard this quote in the past I would often roll my eyes, because it sounded too idealistic. Now I understand what it means. "Be the change you want to see in the world." I am a work in progress.

DR. DENEIA Y. FAIRWEATHER is New York raised and New England educated. Currently based in Tampa, FL, she owns of ESE Consulting, LLC, an educational consultant company that offers professional development for educators of gifted and learning disabled students and a social emotional curriculum called Anthropology in Motion™© (AIM) for students. Dr. Fairweather graduated from the University of South Florida with a M.Ed. in education and a Ph.D. in applied cultural anthropology. Her research focuses on the educational experiences of Black males in the United States and the Caribbean. In her personal life, Dr. Fairweather is a lifelong learner, a mother, and a part-time yogi. She enjoys stimulating conversations, travel, laughter, and a great meal.

41

Enjoying The Ride

GEISEL CHECO
Thirty-six, Dominican

This part of my life, here and now, is what I call enjoyment. You may have that description attached to your twenties, but for me, the thirties are a true joy.

To catch you up, I am about to hit thirty-seven, a father of three boys, and married to my best friend since I was twenty-eight years old. So my thirties got me married and with a first-born little person.

We lived overseas on another Caribbean island where I worked for a local construction company. I say another island because I was born on one, the Dominican Republic. Therefore, my first son was born of two Dominican parents in Trinidad & Tobago. Three years later, we decided to have a second child, but in the middle of it, I decided not to renew my contract, so we went back home.

Being an engineer with two children, and getting back into the labor market after five years being overseas was a bumpy ride to say the least. I got a job, which I lost in a matter of months due to rough economic times, while at the same time my wife was unemployed due to the pregnancy. Thanks to my experience in the field, I got another job a few days later, but it required me to be away from home every so often.

As if two little boys were not enough, we got preggo again for a third time! And with it, I was transferred to Haiti for a high-profile project that required a project manager with my expertise. Being a Dominican in Haiti is not easy due to some business that happened over 170 years ago, but we cannot forget our past or our history. Even though the project was very demanding and going out for drinks was not an option, I decided to write a book on my own. I blog about my real and imaginary life, but to write a book is something else.

So between chapters of my stay in Haiti, I had the concept of what I wanted to write about but never set my foot down to finish it. Until one day I read about a contest for writers in Spanish with an opportunity to have your digital book printed in paperback by a well-renowned publisher. By that time I was operations manager, handling five projects simultaneously.

I started writing the book at 3 a.m. due to a heavy workload (two of the five projects were approaching completion and required extra hours to meet the deadline). I would get home, take a bath, and start singing, "It's three a.m. I must be lonely" (all rights lie with Matchbox Twenty), and then start to write my own piece.

It took me a month to finally have my book presentable, or so I like to think, or maybe it was because the deadline was fast approaching. I rushed to my laptop, in the middle of my working day, with my boss and the Minister of Education present on the job site and I minded my own business. I had to work like that, or not at all.

In the end, I did not even make it into the top five finalists, but I wrote a digital book, in a month, not sleeping, and with lots of responsibilities on my shoulders. I am aiming to print the book on my own and sell it in bookstores all over the Dominican Republic.

And that's why I say that my thirties are about enjoyment, even with all the ups and downs. If these experiences had happened while I was in my twenties, I probably would have ended up divorced, stressed out in my professional life, and definitely without a book that I wrote from scratch.

So I'm inspiring you to not turn thirty but to embrace it, wish it, and dream it. It is the start of a ride to enjoying life to its fullest!

GEISEL CHECO is a morning person, sunset collector, lover of good wine, golf, and antiques, habano's savorer, full moon contemplator, father of three, brother of two, proud son, creator of stories, both real and imaginary. He blogs at www.entrelapizypapel. blogspot.com and is the author of *El Presidente de la Nación*, available on Amazon.

- To the Girl I Once Was -

NENA UBANI A.K.A. DUCHESS
Thirty-four, Nigerian

I spent my teenage years and my twenties trying so hard to fit in. My energy should have been spent more productively. Now, in my early thirties, I feel the most comfortable with myself and sometimes wonder: If I were given a chance to communicate with the girl I once was, what would I tell her?

> To the girl I once was:
> If I had a chance to meet you
> I would tell you to chill
> Life is not a competition
> Do not put too much pressure on yourself
> Aspire to be happy and do the things you love
> It's impossible to please people all the time
> Beauty truly comes from within, so it's okay to go out without makeup sometimes
> Designer bags and shoes are not investments
> Keeping up with trends does not define you
> True friends love you just as you are
> Fulfillment comes from living the life you want
> A life of laughs, love, and spirituality.

NENA UBANI A.K.A. DUCHESS is a UK-based vegan chef, wellness coach, and founder of Igbokwenu Radio, Uziiza.com, and Igbo Women Awards. Radio and TV personality, writer, and talent manager. Nena worked in conjunction with the Metropolitan Police London as a youth mentor, engaging young people as a way to combat crime. She continues to do her work with dignity, representing the African woman wherever she goes.

Blooming Like a Lotus Flower

IVY RUEDA DIEDERICHS
Thirty-two, Colombian

When I was preparing myself, mostly mentally, to turn thirty, a friend of mine told me that her thirties had been the best time of her life. I am still waiting for that. It has been a roller coaster, primarily as I work on becoming comfortable in my own skin (mentally, physically, emotionally, spiritually), and dealing with societal expectations of how my life should be at this point—settled down in my own place, married with kids, contentedly employed, and knowing what I want to do with my life. That's a lot, and I don't fit any of the prescribed categories.

I think the biggest lesson learned for me is picking my battles and understanding that I don't have to be responsible for everything and everyone. I have become a ball of worry and I hate it. I know deep inside I am a free spirit, and I am struggling to find myself again, especially after going through an anxiety meltdown two years ago. That particular episode took an unimaginable toll on me, and while I know I have progressed a lot since then, I am still fighting it, even when I don't show it. It is a process—one I am hoping will become easier with time—because living like this is exhausting, to say the least.

I don't want to end this on a sad note, so I will say this: Don't be afraid of the thirties. Every age brings its good and bad, and all we can do is embrace it, learn from it, and become a better person as a result. That's my goal right now, to be a better person every day.

IVY RUEDA DIEDERICHS is Colombian. Striving every day to be a better daughter, sister, friend, and citizen of the world. Learning to appreciate all that life throws her way, petals and thorns included.

- Chains and Lessons of Strength -

MARISELA PÉREZ
Thirty-two, Nicaraguan

I started working at fifteen for the sake of my family, my siblings first, later for my children. At twenty-one, I had to go to another country illegally to find my sister. We didn't know where she was and seeing my mother cry made me go. I came back with my sister, but while I was there I saw life in a different way. It was tough not being with my family, but I liked it, because I had started working.

I quit school for health issues, so I was working and helping my mother with the kids. I felt different from my siblings. I felt they needed more support than me.

I also got married that year. He started working, and then he changed. He told me things that destroyed my self-esteem and we got divorced. He told me that he got a young woman pregnant, and that he had to take responsibility, because otherwise he would go to jail. I was so naive that I gave him the divorce to prevent him from going to jail. But later, he started to turn it all on me, making me feel guilty, saying that I betrayed him.

I was twenty-four, with one child, when we divorced. I accepted the divorce also because he was abusing me. Since I had been pregnant, he abused me and I thought that's what marriage was about. But I didn't like when he started abusing my child. So I finally said, "No." My family was also getting involved and I didn't want to get them in trouble. They are the most important thing to me.

I changed and found another job, but I was afraid, because he followed me and abused me everywhere he saw me.

Later that year of my divorce, I met the father of my second child, and things went wrong again. This man had a drinking problem, but I was already pregnant, so there was nothing I could do.

I guess I made two mistakes, because I was not that in love with him. He wanted to do the same thing that my first husband did, and I said to myself, "No, I already went through all this." After having my second child, I was alone for a long time because I was afraid to meet someone like that again, and sometimes people fool me. They seem different than what they turn out to be. God was always there when I made the wrong decision. I felt I had to stay with these men, but at the same time, I knew that if I stayed, they could kill me one day. I didn't want to get my family into trouble. I have a violent brother, and I just wanted to be at peace, so my solution was to leave. Sometimes I feel like I ran away from the problem.

Something happened to me when I was in San José in 2007. My brother was killed in Costa Rica, and I was alone. I had started to work three days before, and I received a phone call saying my brother was dead. I didn't know where he was. I never saw him when he was alive. They told me to go the police station. I went at 9 pm. They told me he was at Ciudad Quezada, three hours away from San José, so I had to go back. Even to my mother, I was the weakest one, and now I see that I've done tough things: going to the morgue, to the police, alone. I came back alone. I was so tired that I fell on my knees. I was scared after everything happened, but I still did it all.

I have been with my current and third partner for six years and it is all the same. I'm confused about loving him, because of how he treats me lately. I don't deserve the way he treats me, because I'm not a bad woman. He is jealous, and his mother is too. I don't blame him, but I don't have to accept the way he treats me. But I am afraid to meet someone like that again. I think it is a chain, because the three of them did whatever they wanted. I don't want my children to see that. My youngest child saw it, because my partner did something very bad in front of him.

My partner drinks a lot. Now he is drinking less because I told him I would leave if he didn't stop, and he doesn't want me to leave. He wants to change, but our lives are so complicated. I spend the day in my house with my children and then I go to his place to do his laundry and sleep there, because he doesn't want to live with me. The next morning, I go to my house and make breakfast… that's my life. I guess I've lost the courage to leave. I have my children.

I like my job in the cigar industry. I never knew how to roll. I like the work environment and how employees are treated, because in other places it is not the same. I like to be treated well, maybe because of all I've been through.

MARISELA PÉREZ is the mother of two boys, always living on the edge, smiling no matter the circumstances.

45

Relationship with Myself

MARIA MECHEVA
Thirty-two, Bulgarian

The best is yet to come. I am a firm believer that life begins after thirty when you have high self-awareness, have discovered what you want, and know how to achieve it. I turned thirty, waited for the miracle to happen, for a sudden change to happiness. I didn't think it would take any effort to get there.

I have often asked myself: "What is the key to happiness?" I've always tried to do the right thing, behave the way others expected me to, and be a good girl. I had a good job and wonderful friends, and was doing most of the things I always wanted to, but I felt like something was missing. Buying something nice or going on an exciting trip was just a temporary solution. I was telling myself that those things would make me happy, while I was really waiting for something to happen. I was not giving myself time to enjoy what I had just gotten, and I was immediately chasing after the next thing that would make me feel complete, but it never did. I was successful but very demanding of myself, always wanting to be perfect. Aiming to comply with society's expectations and depending on what others thought, I was missing lots of joyful moments. I liked my life and was sure that happiness depended on things like achievements, the right person to complete me, and staying "cool." But after turning thirty, I started asking myself: "Why doesn't it work?"

I needed to discover what would really make me happy, something completely different from all the things I have done before. Maybe even something I was afraid of. I went to a painting course along the ocean. I have always avoided painting because I thought I was not talented enough and I set high expectations for the final results. I was crying the whole time I painted my first picture. A lot of hidden emotions came out in the process, and by the end of the course, I made a discovery. What is important for me is to dive into the exciting process of creating without focusing on the result. Another great lesson revealed itself when I started giving paintings to my friends. I got wonderful feedback, not because my pictures were perfect, but because I made them wholeheartedly for each person.

So the journey to my inner self began. I started discovering new things, some requiring that I overcome or change old habits, or do a thing I thought I never would. I felt like a child who plays, enjoys every moment, and doesn't care what others think. I felt guilty that I hadn't been in touch with my spontaneous inner child and instead focused on external things, right and wrong.

The key is to have a healthy and true relationship with myself, and embrace the curious child who does things wholeheartedly, believing anything is possible. "Love yourself," echoed in my head for days. I had read it in books before, but it was just a phrase. This time it is my epiphany, a feeling that fills me up. I realized it is the solid base inside me that happiness rests upon. The relationship with myself is the most difficult and interesting, requiring constant care to flourish. Accepting myself with all the good and bad makes me feel complete and free.

I know there is a lot more to discover. Finding myself is a long journey and my first step was daring to fix the relationship with myself.

Now I am not afraid of change. I am grateful for all the wonderful things and people in my life. I do everything wholeheartedly. I enjoy all the little things that make me feel good.

The best is yet to come.

Born and raised in Bulgaria, **MARIA MECHEVA** considers herself a citizen of the world who loves traveling and broadening her horizons. She likes activities that awaken creativity and believes the most valuable way to spend her time is in conversation with friends, sharing moments, thoughts, and experiences.

46

Dream as If You'll Live Forever Live as If You'll Die Tomorrow -

CAROLINA SANTURIAN
Thirty-two, Argentine

The thirties, or the third floor, *la flor de la edad*, represent more than a number to every woman. As we approach this age, I believe most of us find ourselves in a state of anxiety that we have not experienced before. We are concerned with how to keep up with society's standards after leaving our fabulous twenties. Supposedly, this age is when we make money, progress in our professional careers, and decide, as the clock is ticking, whether or not to have kids (assuming we have already found love and gotten married). It's overwhelming. I don't think I fit in this age.

When I was a kid, people in their thirties were old. I couldn't picture myself that age. I saw myself married at the maximum age of twenty-seven, knowing I wanted to be a young mom. Today, I am thirty-two and none of those things have happened. The one thing I dream of every day is getting married, but kids are on another level. I love kids, but there is more to it.

I am originally from Argentina and I moved to the US in 2002. I graduated cum laude at Barry University with a degree in advertising. During my college years, I met wonderful people who became close friends. I had the opportunity to work at MTV Latin America, which still sounds like a dream to me. Then last year, I became a realtor. I never thought I would be capable of moving to a country so far away from mine and earning a degree in a different language, but here I am.

At the sweet age of twenty-eight, four days away from a trip to Europe with my family, I was diagnosed with breast cancer. The doctor gave me the results in front of my dad and boyfriend, with no "verbal anesthesia," the coldest way one can speak to a human being. I froze. My first thought was, "I am going to die." My dad's reaction was several times stronger, the reaction of a father seeing his little girl suffer. He wanted to punch that doctor hard in the face. My boyfriend reacted in the most practical way, asking what we needed to do to get rid of the cancer. Meanwhile, I remained silent. The doctor wanted to perform a double mastectomy. That's when my dad asked him for all the results and we walked out the door.

I called my gynecologist in Argentina and we flew the day after to see him. In less than ten days, I had a lumpectomy instead, as it was unnecessary to remove the whole breast. As soon as I recovered from surgery, I came back to the US for treatment. I went through eight rounds of chemo, followed by six weeks of radiation.

Not to brag, but I think of how brave I was. I lost my long red hair, eyebrows and lashes, gained so much weight, and felt so tired and nauseated, but I still managed to beat cancer. What kept me alive was love. The love of my family, boyfriend, dog, and friends did wonders for my healing process. I don't think I'd be here today if it weren't for them. Despite the immense sorrow, they would put on their best faces every day and stayed by my side when I needed them most. My dad shaved his head for me. One of my friends donated her hair twice in my honor to make wigs for other people fighting cancer. My dog licked my bald head every morning in an attempt to make my hair grow back. My mom gave up her life in Argentina for six months to be by my side, and no words can describe what my sisters mean to me, my most precious treasures.

My boyfriend saved my life, not only because he was the one who found the lump, but because he is the man of my dreams. He deals with my extremely hot temper, makes me laugh, and loves my dog and me like no one else ever could. He is the one who does everything to make me happy and who I know I will marry one day.

The saying, "What doesn't kill you makes you stronger" comes to mind. Having been diagnosed with breast cancer at twenty-eight, and being alive now to tell the story—well, I am one tough cookie. I find myself more sensitive and vulnerable than before. I don't know if it's the cancer or the thirties, or something else, but my heart feels a lot softer. My respect, compassion, and love for animals have grown immensely, and I dream of someday owning a huge farm where I can take care of all the animals that need a loving home. I feel more nostalgic, and I am not a fan of passing time. Time flies and life was created to be lived, so I learned to do the things I love and enjoy every minute of it.

My grandfather used to say all the time, "Problems are part of life: Some are bigger than others, but they will always accompany you wherever you go." The trick is to give the right amount of importance to each of them, something I work on daily. I am a very anxious person, and tend to worry about things before they ever happen. I've been like that for a long time, so I know changing the way I think will be a lifelong endeavor.

As a breast cancer survivor with no history of breast cancer in my family, I now strongly believe in the connection of mind and body. Fear, anger, hate, and envy are feelings that take us to a bad place. My cancer was brought about by repressed feelings from my childhood and how I used to look at life, which is a whole different story. We are what we think. I am positive about that.

Your mind can either save you or kill you.

I got my hair back, and was able to take that trip to Europe a year later. I am still the hot-tempered redhead as always, but with a goal of becoming filled with inner peace, to embrace all the good things God has given me. I look forward to traveling the world, as that is what I love the most, and to living my life with passion. James Dean once said, "Dream as if you'll live forever, live as if you'll die tomorrow." From now on, that is my motto.

Let your thirties look good on you, or better said, let you look good in your thirties!

CAROLINA SANTURIAN was born in Mar del Plata, Argentina in 1981. Moved to Miami in 2002 and has lived there ever since. Stage IV breast cancer survivor (metastasis diagnosed in 2016). She is passionate about animals and strongly supports the cause to stop their abuse. Her family, husband, dog, and friends are the most important things to her. Her ultimate goal is to travel the world and live a happy, healthy life.

47

Everything You Do, Do It with Passion

INEABELLE SOTO
Thirty-seven, Puerto Rican

Back in Puerto Rico, I studied at specialized middle and high schools for the arts. After graduating from college with a bachelor's degree in advertising, I worked for ten years in the advertising field and stopped when I gave birth to my daughter. But I felt the urge to go back to my creative side. I took a brief cake design course and started baking from home. Even though it was something fun to do and business was good (and surprisingly growing), my husband and I felt that we needed to do something bigger than that.

When looking for that "big thing to do," my husband and I started developing what we now call Artsy Hive. We started exploring the possibility of opening a business related to our background in the arts. That's when we thought of an experience we'd had in a pottery painting place we went to with our daughter and of the things we would do differently. Pottery painting is an old concept and we felt that the options already out there were stuck in that old-fashioned era. When deciding to go for this concept, we wanted people of all ages to get inspired from the moment they stepped inside. We wanted clients to feel comfortable in a space that is not only for kids, but for the entire family. Therefore, while designing the environment, we went for a clean, modern yet cozy shop.

We designed a place that we, as parents, wanted to come back to not only with our family, but also with our adult friends.

It took us a year and a half to open our doors after many good and bad days, stress, and huge decisions. My greatest satisfaction and the second best feeling I have every day (the first is when my daughter comes back from school) is opening Artsy Hive's door, turning on the lights, and putting the music on. I always take a moment to see what we've accomplished. The beauty of the space. I feel in love every single day I come in. We worked so hard to open, and we must work harder to keep it that way, one day at a time.

Artsy Hive has taught me that I am brave. It was not easy to step out of my comfort zone. To wake up every day worried about how this project will change our lives forever and yet keep going forward. I have learned that it is not a decision to be brave. Bravery is already inside of you.

I am a woman, daughter, granddaughter, wife, mother, friend, entrepreneur, creator, immigrant, and active community member, among many other dimensions. I've decided not to wear different hats. I won't stop being a mother to be a wife; I won't stop being a friend to be a woman. The best way to go through life is to apply every single identity in your everyday. While working at Artsy Hive, and in life in general, you must have empathy. We have to use all those facets we have as women in the best way possible. If there is a mom struggling to control her toddler, I will never step back and watch. I will always offer my help and understanding. That's how I manage my own life, using empathy, being humble, and just being human. That's also how I make connections with our clients. It's a win-win.

Now that Artsy Hive is open, my hobby is finding things we can do with our daughter and spending our "free" time with her. Although, I still have a passion for creating things with my hands. When it's just me, Ineabelle, I'm at home and I lie down. I can't nap, I don't know why; I like to just lie down. Netflix and chill, literally. I rest. As simple as that.

Many things have happened and are still happening during the journey of my thirties. I believe that it's been a decade full of findings. My daughter was born when I was almost thirty. My purpose in life changed because of her, and my mind shifted.

I now think that this is the real age to make bold decisions and still have the stamina, energy, and passion to do it (contrary to when I was in college). I thought that having a baby would stop me from doing something that felt like it had to be done. Fear, doubts, concerns, you name it, I feel it all, but I still manage to do everything. I do it with fear; I do it with doubts and concerns. This is my mindset. I believe that in your thirties you are mature enough to visualize yourself in a position and plan the best way to achieve it. Only maturity can make you do that. I call this taking "planned risks."

My tips for other thirtysomethings doing it all like me?

1. Work for what's right and what feels right.

2. Find your passion. Everything you do, do it with passion.

3. I invite everyone to start a relationship with HIM. In my thirties, I received the call and decided to obey. That decision changed my entire life for the best. I'm not a religious person; I just have a relationship with our creator.

4. You are awesome, you are amazing, you are a superwoman, and you are not alone.

INEABELLE SOTO is an artsy Boricua woman, daughter, granddaughter, wife, mother, friend, entrepreneur, creator, immigrant, active community member, among many other dimensions. Based in Miami Shores. Walks by faith, not by sight.

48

From Financier to Makeup Artist

FHARAS SANDOVAL
Thirty-six, Dominican

I already knew that losing sleep for several days in a row was either a very good sign or a very bad sign. My head just would not stop! I knew the risk-return binomial like the freckles on my face, which are many. The first one—risk—seduced me (naughty at last!), and profitability? For someone who thought she had lost everything, it didn't matter.

At that moment, two friends with whom I had small businesses suggested that I try my luck with the "skills" that each of them had noticed in me. I agreed only to keep myself occupied, not because I thought it would be my destiny. Imagine: Fharas doing makeup! Or even worse, waxing!

I had been trained to be organized, disciplined, strong, and constant. I was supposed to study and become a professional, marry and buy a home, get and keep a "decent" job that would help me have a "decent" life and raise my children. Everything in that order. I wish you could see my face of mockery as I write this—I still do not believe it.

My university education was oriented toward quality and customer service. Quickly, my professors noticed certain strengths in me, and thank God, they actually pointed them out. They said if I worked with my talent I could climb the professional ladder. I understood and took advantage of the skills I had—who wants to be average when you can be outstanding?

To be honest, there were no opportunities waiting for me. I created them, and where I could not create them, I could not stay. That's how aggressive I was in all jobs. And of course, that attitude was not well liked by my colleagues and sometimes openly rejected by my superiors. Didn't they understand what I was really worth? @ # *%. I had so many misunderstandings with my co-workers. What I learned is that being good is good, and being "the best" is bad.

I educated myself and then I re-educated myself. I made my way professionally, being a single mother, ambitious, and committed in a society that crucifies you for being one of the three—I was all three. I cannot deny that I received great opportunities; I managed to become a senior executive in a renowned business group and was known as *Doña* Fharas. What the… ?! My life revolved around staff meetings, social work commitments, and financial models the size of the universe that I had to memorize and keep positive. It was also not strange for me to receive calls at odd hours with the question, "What is the ROI?"

Suddenly one morning, I opened my eyes. There I was with a partner, children, a pet—but without work. A professional like me! And my only thought, given the low probability of reentering the job market in that situation (I had lost my job and gotten pregnant almost the next day), was that under no circumstances was that going to be the end. On several occasions I was offered work. I accepted a few assignments, but life insisted on returning me to the "warmth of the home," which was more like a kind of infernal bonfire that burned me mercilessly.

I learned to value family time. I learned to love time for myself. I did things that I knew very well how to do, but that I hated, such as cooking and belonging to the parents' club of my children's school, and even that I began to value. While this was going on, my real self, wrapped in an impetuous air of "entrepreneurship," kidnapped a room in my apartment and turned it into an impromptu waxing and makeup studio. Like a good financier, I cut expenses and invested them in "the project." I wrote down everything in several paper notebooks, opened social network profiles, and went back to school, this time to educate myself in the new field of beauty. I contacted important people in the industry and from the first moment I was once again making my way, making opportunities, and where I could not create them I used my creativity (which I did not know I had). I put all my effort and love into this new challenge and I triumphed.

I want you to know that during this process, I had basically no support from my family and friends (except for my mother-in-law and my friend Pamela). None of my relatives came for my services, and if they did, they wanted everything for free! They hardly recommended me. It was discouraging and kind of unusual, but it did not stop me. I was too ambitious to be distracted. That approach is key for an entrepreneur. Today I can say that my clientele and followers are 100 percent organic, thanks only to Fharas!

It's been a little more than three years since I launched myself in the beauty industry and without trauma, I have managed to maintain forty-one steady clients (30 percent of whom are foreigners). I have on average 5.3 new clients per month, a reputation for excellence, and quality services provided with 86 percent satisfaction. Believe me, these numbers are excellent! To have started from scratch and survived the attempt, this is enough for me. I was never going to stop and follow what others said. Ambition has no limits! And I know that in the game of life, the bet is always on myself. What about you? Are you willing?

FHARAS SANDOVAL is a finance professional, makeup artist by vocation, and entrepreneur by need.

49

— Quinceañera —

WENDY ESPINAL
Thirtysomething, Dominican

Ever since I can remember, I have looked much younger than I am. And you know, a teenager who starts going out will never understand looking "younger" as a great virtue, quite the opposite. It's even worse when other people consider you "a very mature young lady."

When I was of legal age (a term that is a little aspirational for an eighteen-year-old girl), bouncers would ask for my ID, and I would say to myself: "Someday I will use this to my advantage."

That day arrived much sooner than expected. After several existential crises (at twenty-one, twenty-six, and twenty-eight), which are typical of any woman who considers herself to be more than a flower vase in life, I thought that thirty was going to be hard. By the time I had reached my third decade of life, I had already given therapy to many of my friends. I listened, calmed their hysteria, and reminded them that we are in the 21st century, etc. I did all of this while anticipating my own breakdown.

Well, to my surprise, that crisis never came. In fact, I waited for it, anxious, wearing makeup. But I felt exactly the same. I felt calm. Both spiritually and physically, I considered myself "ageless." I didn't feel subjected to any of the social criticism I'd expected. I was just acting as I had before, living life at my own pace. No matter that the acne I never suffered in adolescence had suddenly shown up, my hair was rebelling like a teenage version of Amanda Miguel, or that after four comfortable years of not wearing retainers, my teeth had gradually opened up in the form of a fan (the exact metaphor used by my dentist) and I was suddenly considering yet another round of braces, or that in the romance department, not only did I suffer from Wendy's syndrome (the name is pure coincidence...or is it?), I continued to run into Peter Pans, though after years of self-study and self-criticism, I had reached the undeniable diagnosis that I was also a Peter Pan. I wasn't even stressed out about the long list (mental, in my case) of "Things to do before turning thirty," nor the fact that thanks to the greatest global economic recession of recent times (and especially in the country that had adopted me), all my financial goals had to be significantly revised.

Despite all of this, turning thirty was a special event, and I wanted to celebrate it in a special way (after all, I am quite a social creature and often succumb to social demands, especially parties). After almost five years living outside my country, the Dominican Republic, and five years since I last celebrated my birthday there, I took it as an excuse to swap my Christmas trip for a summer one and receive my thirties there. Conveniently, I still had the dress from my quinceañera and wanted to see if it would fit me. No, I had not kept the dress with that intention, it was just a coincidence. I swear. And no, it was not the typical Latin quinceañera princess like dress, even by then, I had developed special style and taste.

The dress not only fit me, but it looked better. Much better. And there, as I stood in front of the mirror, with thirty years and my quinceañera dress on, I reached the epicenter of that inevitable reflection about turning thirty: fifteen years later, it was still the exact same me, the same curious, sensitive, and restless little woman, with the look of an eternal explorer, a big smile, a sturdy body and a head full of crazy curls, ideas, and questions—okay, my hair was even more wild since I'd been freed from the Dominican imposition of straightening my hair—and there was my brain, and my strong hands, my back, and my somewhat more delicate heart (after a few stumbles and lost loves), my still restless feet, tired from so many paths explored, with a few fallen heroes and a few broken dreams (but more to fulfill)… Yes, it was the same me… and maybe even improved.

I wrote the above paragraphs six years ago. They were overflowing with innocence and unfinished, like many things I have started in my life. But then Laura contacted me and I was able to finish this essay just in time. It was therapy and a gift. A gift that makes me recall—through smiles and tears—the many experiences, reflections, dreams, self-criticisms, attempts, fantasies, successes, mistakes, and comebacks that I have lived in my thirty-something years. Therapy, without a doubt.

Today, I am closer to forty than thirty, but I still look much younger than I am. The big difference is that now I don't obsess about the next crisis, or whether I still fit into that dress from my quinceañera. Now I face the real "mambo," with my hormones fooling around and my memory failing; with almost always being the oldest in the group; with increasingly frightening medical visits and my ovarian reserve challenging me with its countdown; with distances that feel longer and longer; with less intense illusion and less important dreams; with the lack of loved ones that have left me and the inevitable reversal of the role of mother; with the love that does not end up staying, the scattering increasing and the willpower decreasing… Now a few more items have been added to the backpack of life.

Luckily, others help balance the load: the privilege and serenity of being able to continue choosing the life I want, the certainty that home and warmth are carried inside, and the inexhaustible force of a well-sown root, well cared for and well-loved.

Oh! And that the dress still fits me.

WENDY ESPINAL, is a Dominican producer and documentary filmmaker based between Santo Domingo and Spain. Her work is built on research, process, and meaning. Her professional experience includes international film, entertainment, and cultural productions in the Dominican Republic, Europe, and the United States, believing in arts and culture as tools for change. Her work as a filmmaker has been supported by Programa Ibermedia, Fonprocine Dominican Republic, Berlinale Talents Guadalajara, Iberdoc, UN Women, MiradasDoc, Directed by Women, and other international organizations and film festivals. *The Surrounding World*, her most recent documentary film, premiered at the Havana International Film Festival in 2019, and reflects on the evolving images and sounds of the rural Dominican landscape.

50

Recap

TUTI LOOR
Thirty-eight, Ecuadorian

The fact that I get to write about my thirties as a "looking back at" more than a "now that I am" is funny to me. I really don't feel this old. I'm thirty-eight, but, except for the few times when I wake up with a new ache, most of the time I feel like I'm still twenty-three. I dress in jeans and t-shirts and wear sneakers. I don't have kids and I still don't do well with responsibility and commitment.

Being in my thirties is equally good or even better than being in my twenties. Now I know who I am and what I want. Maybe I don't have everything figured out, but I know that much. I have fewer friends, but better ones. My favorite part is I really don't care what people think of me anymore.

Being a TV producer, here is my "recap" of the last eight years (from the time I turned thirty until today):
- I had my first long-term relationship (nine years and counting).
- I was let go from my job for the first time.
- I sold everything I had, got a backpack and traveled through England, Egypt, Jordan, India, Nepal, Thailand, and Cambodia.
- I let my hair grow back again (I had shaved it for two years before that).
- I spent two lazy weeks in the Galapagos Islands.
- I lived in the Florida Keys for two years.
- I wore my gray hair proudly.
- I got my first boat.
- I sold my first boat.
- I sold my car and motorcycle, got an RV, and drove all the way to Alaska.
- I lived in Alaska for four months.
- I drove the RV back to the Keys.
- I went to the Sundance Film Festival for the first time.
- I bought a house with a yard.
- I got my first tattoo.

So if you are one of those people who think somehow your youth ends at thirty… well, I have to go get ready for my cruise around the Mediterranean. Peace!

TUTI LOOR is a world traveler, storyteller, animal lover, and more importantly... cleverly disguised as a responsible adult.

51

- Me At 38 -

ANA KARINA CESPEDES
Thirty-eight, Peruvian

Free of the burden of me
Of the need to fulfill every desire
To fill every hole
To find all the pieces in this puzzle
A puzzle I never could control

Free to just be
To let go and let the pieces fall into place
To truly believe in myself
To not just repeat what I now know
But to feel it intensely in my bones

Free to make the right decisions
Without consulting the world
Free of stupid thoughts and able
To listen to my voice, my thoughts, my heart

Free because I don't need anyone
I simply want to share my life with everyone
Embracing all the love that surrounds me

Free to finally be me
Gray hair, wrinkles, and fat
You couldn't pay me to go back

This feeling has no price
It's not for sale, there's no negotiating

Free to roam, free to love, free to leave it all behind.

I've never felt freer, more creative, or more confident in my life. We gain this as we get older and as long as we are open to change for the better, we will. I'm even excited to be forty, because I know it can get only better. It hasn't been a bed of roses. I'm twice-divorced, lost my front tooth, and have a step-daughter who went through cancer. My childhood was tainted by abuse, but somewhere deep in my heart, I knew things could only get better. In spite of everything dark in my life, I believed in the light at the end of the tunnel.

It's important to hang in there, have good people in your life, and most of all, listen to your gut. It takes practice, but the sooner you can develop that skill—fine-tune your voice—it will keep you from making terrible mistakes.

We have the answer to all our issues. We just need to learn to listen to God and ourselves. He gives us signs every second of the day. I promise. We just need to keep our eyes, ears, minds, and hearts open.

ANA KARINA CESPEDES is Peruvian-born, Miami-raised, world-based. Accepts the never-ending task of becoming a better version of herself. Looks forward to the lesson she is here to learn, and to sharing that knowledge with the next generation of women.

52

EVA HART
Thirty-nine, Dominican

Today I turn 39. I have lived more in my thirties than in my whole life before them.

I gave birth to my second son. Later, I lost the 40 pounds that I gained during the pregnancy.

I learned how to surf and developed a special bond with nature and the ocean.

A year and a half later I got divorced and began a new life as a single mother. A family of three.

I got to catch up with social life and a lot of dating I didn't do before getting married.

In my early thirties I started a spiritual journey with meditation and yoga. I moved to a new country with my sons and tried starting a multicultural family with a foreign partner. It didn't work out as planned and as a result we ended the relationship.

I reconnected with the love of my life, a guy that I had dated right after getting divorced the first time, and it seems this time we were ready for each other.

During this decade I restarted my business from scratch in a new country. I became a filmmaker, and I worked on my introversion, as part of growing a business was to network and promote my brand.

I founded Dupla, a side business with my partner. I learned how to network and hustle in a new language.

I went back to basics teaching my oldest son how to draw and reconnected with my passion for painting.

Throughout my thirties I learned to set boundaries, realized I can't make everybody happy, and learned to put myself first. I learned to say no. I learned to be transparent.

EVA HART has nearly twenty years of experience as a director and photographer in the advertising and fashion worlds. She has worked for national and international brands and publications in the Dominican Republic and United States. She is a graduate of IDEP BARCELONA, a professional school for graphic design, fashion, and photography. In 2012, she successfully transitioned into film and has been working as a director and cinematographer for music videos, shorts, TV commercials, and documentaries. She co-produced an episode of NHAP Zoom featuring Laura Gómez of *Orange Is the New Black*. She also created DOBEDO Miami, a documentary series of inspiring Miami residents. She calls Miami Beach home.

53

My Thirties: A Birthday Journal

CAROLE KHATCHADOURIAN DUFOUR
Thirty-nine, French

Within a week, I will say goodbye to my thirties. Nine years have mixed pain with joy, but the happiness has been real. And so I share my birthday memories.

I am 30!

It is a drunken birthday night, surrounded by friends. This year is the beginning of my new love story with Chris. The storm finally passed, and it made us stronger, invincible even. My first daughter Leah is four years old and I am thirty! I feel good, but the most important thing for me is to save my marriage and family.

I can now say that I did just that.

31st Birthday: With Chris and friends, celebrating outdoors with a smile!

32nd Birthday: A turning point in my life

I'm pregnant, again, a second little girl will come to beautify our life. I'm happy, plus we are leaving the Paris region to head southwest to Bordeaux and the beaches.

33rd Birthday: We are now based in Teich

We found a house that we landscaped to our taste, and life is beautiful. We are now a family of four, since Roxane was born on August 17th.

34th Birthday: Destination Mykonos

We are vacationing on this beautiful island for my birthday. It is our first time going as a couple, without the children. It is a dream week, with a romantic restaurant birthday night. I love my Chris!

35th Birthday: Three Generations

My mom is always by my side to guide me.

36th Birthday: Fiesta with friends at home

I met Anne, Val, and Cedric in the southwest, and Sam and Laetitia in the Nile. Thank you destiny!

37th Birthday: Lacanau, a ritual

I am enjoying my favorite little restaurant with my favorite friends, Cilou and Greg, sheer happiness.

38th Birthday: Evening at home with lots of new friends: Myriam, Alex, Hélène, and Pierre

I have been spoiled with gifts.

39th Birthday: Back at Lacanau with friends Cilou and Greg

My daughters are my pride, my strength, and my reason to live. They are my fight every day.

This year, I turn forty and life is still beautiful.

And finally a little message for the one who accompanies me every day and makes my life so enjoyable: I love you!

CAROLE KHATCHADOURIAN DUFOUR was born and raised in France. Traded Paris for a smaller beach town with a better quality of life. A high school teacher to hundreds, mother of two, in love with The One for the past thirty+ years. Passionate about cooking, traveling, and spending time with friends.

54

A New Cycle

ALFONSINA FERREIRA†
Thirty-nine, Dominican

"My shining thirty-nine" is what I have chosen to call this new cycle. I reread pages written during the most intense months I have lived, with my naked heart, a soul full of faith, and every cell in my body bursting with divine love. Those months were the most enriching, revealing, and transcendental.

Memories of what happened only a year ago bring tears to my eyes as I write this. I remember preparing, physically and mentally, emotionally and spiritually, for the moment that would mark a rebirth in my life: surgery that would put an end to my battle against cancer. The "battle" was more than cancer. It was against my ego, my paradigms, my mistaken beliefs, conversations that did not support me, and, most of all, against all that stood in the way of finding the best version of myself, my essence, my true self.

Since then, many things have happened: expected miracles and unexpected blessings, immeasurable manifestations of the most genuine and pure love, and the hint on the horizon of a new future, which goes beyond what I could ever imagine. Today, days away from the beginning of the last cycle of my thirties, I walk the path of life with the deepest gratitude, ushering in a new and exciting chapter. I am filled with great plans, ideas, hopes, dreams, and goals. And I have a new purpose: to be.

Yes, to just be.

Be what I want to be, heedless of those little voices that tell me I cannot. Be what I can be, leaving aside the strenuous and insufficient efforts of wanting to fit in and please anyone but myself. But more than anything, be what I came to be: light, love, peace, and contribution. I will always remember the immense privilege I have to open my eyes every morning, breathe, and realize life has given me a new opportunity: the gift of living a new day.

Born in Santo Domingo to a loving family, **ALFONSINA FERREIRA** showed her interest in serving and contributing as a child. She had more than twenty years of experience in banking and business, and a master's degree in business administration. When she turned thirty, the experience of personal growth through transformation and leadership workshops inspired her to obtain a certification in coaching, as well as to become certified as a Transformational Trainer in the LTDG Academy (Leadership Training & Development Group). At age thirty-seven, she faced what would be the biggest challenge of her life: the diagnosis of breast cancer, which she embraced and received as an opportunity to reinvent herself and learn as much as possible. In her final years, she pursued a certification as a health coach with the Integrative Institute for Nutrition in New York, so that she could share her healing experience and support others in creating well-being, love, and happiness in their lives. Her sisters continue sharing her legacy through her Instagram page, @happy_healthy_ways.

55

Forty Life Lessons

YAHIRA POLANCO
Thirty-nine, Dominican

Today I begin my challenge of sharing forty lessons that I have learned in life, considering the fact that in forty days I will be forty:

1. Being yourself is the best way to live. Authentic people do not always fit in, but we are happier. I love being who I am.

2. Life works like a boomerang: Everything that we do, good and bad, comes back to us with the same intensity.

3. You can always start over. Sometimes we give up too quickly and that is why we leave behind unrealized goals and unfulfilled dreams.

4. Something I have learned about the upbringing of our children is to respect their essence, guide them down the path of good, and teach them values—but without wanting to change them. As parents, the challenge is to educate them by loving them just as they are.

5. When one begins to mature, she learns that happiness is not eternal. That is why I have learned over time to recognize those fleeting moments in which I am happy and enjoy them to the fullest. I value them when they arrive and I thank God for the blessings with which he rewards me.

6. Motherhood, from my point of view, is one of the most difficult challenges in the world. But if I have learned anything about being a happy mother, it's that I must first be a happy woman. Sometimes, because we want to fulfill our stereotyped roles of the perfect mother, we forget ourselves and end up being perfectly bitter mothers. I am a woman, wife, and mother and I try to dedicate time to all three.

7. Not everything is black or white. We must learn to see the gray tones of life: It will not always be all or nothing. When we understand that, we take pressure off our lives.

8. We should keep passing through stages and living each moment of our lives fully. We cannot stay frozen in time, longing for the past. Each stage has its charm and we cannot look at things with the same eyes as we did long ago.

9. I read this and loved it: "A ship in harbor is safe-but that is not what ships are built for." John A. Shedd. And that's the way it is. We're afraid to leave our comfort zone and undertake new paths, new challenges, or simply live new experiences. We have to take risks. It's scary, but worse is that over time we wonder what would have happened if we had done this or that.

10. It is difficult, but one must avoid being surrounded by negative people—people

who have a problem for each solution and who find the negative side of everything. They steal your energy, stress you out, and, worst of all, do not contribute anything to your life.

11. Life has a thousand ways to teach us and not all are pleasant. One of the greatest lessons of my life came from what I thought at the time was the worst thing that could happen to me. Now, a few months later, I can say that what I learned not only made me a better human being but also encouraged me to look around and value everything.

12. We should all cultivate a hobby, be it reading, cooking, writing, collecting, sewing, fishing, filmmaking, embroidery, or making crafts. I have several, but I recognize that I am lacking determination and perseverance when it comes to hobbies, so I am dedicating myself more fully to these activities in the new year. This is one of the main tasks on my list of happiness.

13. In order to jump you have to let go. We cannot stay tied to things, places, or people who no longer fulfill a purpose in our lives.

14. Many times we do not agree with the decisions of our friends or families, but we must always respect the fact that people think differently than we do.

15. We cannot walk through life sowing apples and be surprised that we do not harvest pears. Sometimes we want things from life—from others, from jobs, from school, from relationships—things we do not strive for and especially things we did not give. As the old saying goes, "Whatever a man sows, that he will also reap."

16. As Ruben Blades says, "Family is family and love is love." I have always loved my family, but with the passage of time I have learned to value and love them even more. I thank God for the blessing of having a true family that has accompanied, understood, and supported me in each stage of my life!

17. In parenting matters, I have learned that nobody has a perfect formula. Each family educates from their point of view, from their intimate conviction that what they are doing is the best. So I do not judge, I do not voice my opinion, and I do not evaluate the parenting practices of anyone.

18. Our real life goes way beyond appearances. We are bent on pretending and we forget to live for real (I admit that I include myself in this category). We do not do anything without wanting to leave a record in our social networks, of course, as long as they are things that attract attention and generate likes. On my list of happiness, I have also included a wish to live for real again.

19. Always having a project to do or a dream to fulfill is like a booster. It helps us keep going forward and gives us hope. When day-to-day routines overwhelm us, thinking about the project we want to complete makes us feel better. It does not always have to be something big. It can be as small as losing five pounds, redecorating an area of the house, taking a trip, learning to do something new, or getting a new car. Projects that we plan and execute little by little give us so much satisfaction when we finally conquer them. I always have one in the folder!

20. Letting things flow is one of my biggest challenges. I get frustrated when I cannot control things. From experience I can say that it only produces stress, discomfort, and even wrinkles.

21. From the outside, the domino game is always easy. We are experts in fixing the situations of others, but rarely apply those same guidelines or solutions to ourselves. Putting ourselves in someone else's place, and seeing things from their point of view, is important when giving an opinion or advice.

22. All my life I've heard my mom say, "Nobody can give what they do not have." That's a truth bigger than a temple. Sometimes we hope to get things that will never be possible simply because they are not configured either in our mind or in our heart.

23. Our children, without intending it, are an inexhaustible source of wisdom. If you were to ask me what I learned from my Lia, I would say to never give up. Since she was little, she has been very persistent in her goals. When she does not achieve something, I have seen her get sad, but I've never seen her give up.

24. The biggest lesson I've learned from my Evita Lunera is how happy you can be when you're free, when you're not tied to stereotypes, and you give yourself the opportunity to express yourself. Guiding her along the road of life has been a challenge for me, but I cannot deny that I enjoy seeing the pleasure it gives her to feel free. Some may not understand me, but I feel it!

25. Problems have to be solved at the right moment. The longer we wait, the more complicated things get.

26. There is a message that I have read many times: "Bloom where God plants you." Regardless of circumstances, our mission is to bear fruit, leave traces, and try to be an example.

27. A lesson I learned from my little boy: Being grateful for everything, appreciating the little things, and above all understanding the strength of a mother's heart.

28. When we fail we must learn to apologize. It is never easy to recognize that we are wrong because sometimes we fail unconsciously, but we must always be humble and ask for forgiveness. I recognize that this is one of the lessons I need to keep learning.

29. I humbly believe that the worst mistake parents can make is to blind ourselves to recognizing the weaknesses of our children. Sometimes something in our heart tells us that things are not going well (in their development, in their socialization, in how they treat others, in their self-esteem, in short, in any aspect) and we prefer to ignore the situation. We justify it, blame others, but we never face it, and that, in my opinion, is the worst thing we can do to our children. Instead we should help them solve anything that affects them intellectually, physically, or emotionally. This is my primary goal as a mother.

30. There comes a time in life when we must stop depending on our parents and I do not mean financially. I mean taking charge of our lives, our decisions, our welfare, and overcoming those things that affect us mentally and emotionally. We have to grow!

31. We can call it intuition, the sixth sense, a hunch, vibes, foreboding, etc., but the truth is that I have learned with the wisdom only years can give to follow the inner voice that warns me when something is positive or negative. The interesting thing is that it is always, always correct!

32. I cannot finish this journey without thinking about one of the most influential people in my life: my mom. If I had to summarize her lessons in two words, they would be, "Be strong." She never told me outright, but she has preached it by example since I was very young. She taught me to overcome obstacles no matter how hard I think they are. She taught me without knowing it that strength comes from within us, and that there are times when rising from the depths is our only option.

33. There comes a time when we learn to enjoy the little things in life and understand that there lies our much-desired happiness. Spend a fantastic weekend without too much planning and without too many things. Thank God for everything.

34. It takes a lot of work, but sometimes we have to let our children fail to learn their lesson. We can guide them and give them advice, but we cannot figure out their life. They might not understand now, but when they grow up, they will be grateful that we taught them to fend for themselves.

35. It has taken me a long time to learn to yield, to give up reason, to give up space. But I have learned that not all battles have to be fought, much less won. As the saying goes, sometimes losing is winning.

36. A fundamental part of the process of building and maintaining a relationship (be it with a partner, friend, child, or colleague) is the details, and I am not talking about expensive gifts. I am referring to small demonstrations of affection, of gratitude, of solidarity, and reminding others how important they are in our lives. I am a person who focuses on details and this is one of the skills I try to teach others.

37. In recent years, I have begun to set my own parameters and my own canons. I've started to ignore the expectations of others and to rule only by mine. I've learned to live as Sinatra did: My Way.

38. A good friend once told me: "You cannot run more than the ball." Not long ago I learned that this is a big truth stated simply. We cannot anticipate events or everything that should be done. Things in life have their own time and no matter how hard we run, some things are destined to take their time and almost nothing happens overnight. How difficult it is for some of us to understand this.

39. Sometimes you have to take off the Wonder Woman cape, admit that you are not as strong as everyone believes, recognize that sometimes life is just too much, and that we cannot do everything—just like today!

40. I finish this list with one of the most important lessons I have learned: Nothing gives more satisfaction in life than knowing that you have done things well, that when the day is over you are sure that in all the roles you have to play you gave 100 percent, and

especially that you can go to bed at peace with yourself.

YAHIRA POLANCO is a woman, wife, mother of three, privileged daughter, younger sister, and friend who loves life and enjoys it with the heart. #Simple.

56

— *Letting Go* —

ANA KARINA CESPEDES
Thirty-nine, Peruvian

My thirties started with a breakup. He and I weren't as compatible as I thought we were when we were in our twenties. I chose to stay with him too many times, always talking myself out of walking out. Afraid to be alone until I finally chose to let him go.

By thirty-one, I was living in my new apartment. I was still reckless with my money and my heart, feeling vulnerable and overly confident at the same time. I was desperately looking for my prince charming, the man of my dreams, the man who would make me his wife, his queen, the mother of his children. I hadn't realized that I needed to become the woman of my dreams first, the queen of my home, the b**** in charge.

And so I became involved with the wrong man... again. And for six years I woke up each day knowing that I was not where I wanted to be and he wasn't the man for me. I hadn't recognized that I had a voice and needed to listen to it—my fear of the unknown was too strong. During those six years, I sought signs everywhere and waited for something to find me, guide me, rescue me.

Turning forty was not something I was looking forward to at that time. I was afraid that I was never going to meet that man or have children. I tormented myself with thoughts like, "My grandmothers are old and they'll never meet my children," and I thought of the women in my family who had never gotten married or had children. They were alone and sad. I was terrified of becoming like them.

When I finally let go of that relationship, I felt like I had reached the surface of the ocean. Like the world had just rolled off my shoulders. I had been carrying all this emotional weight to the point that it had turned physical. I was thirty pounds overweight. I couldn't look at myself in the mirror. I was destroyed. I needed to recharge, urgently.

So I took off to Paris, because why not?

And I had sex with a French man on my thirty-seventh birthday.

And I enjoyed
every
second
of it.

Suddenly, I felt like a kid in a candy store, like I could do anything! So I quit my job of eight years and took off for forty-three days to travel. I went to Italy, Germany, Czech

Republic, Austria, and Hungary. I turned thirty-eight in a club in Bologna getting free vanilla vodka shots from the owner. I danced with the owner of the Firenze train station and was hung over the next morning. And I was happy.

At that time, too, I decided it was time to forgive myself for everything and allow for a clean slate.

By thirty-eight, I was doing a lot. I launched myself as a photographer and couldn't believe how smoothly things started flowing from there. I had four gallery showings within a year. I read a poem in front of an audience. I chose to change my body. I chose to become the best version of myself before I turned forty. I needed a massive makeover: physical, emotional, spiritual, mental, and then some.

Now I'm a few months away from the big 4-0. I haven't found the man of my dreams, but I am the woman of mine. I don't have the children that I had been longing for, but I've allowed myself to be a child again and stand under the sun and breathe the ocean air and drive with the windows down. Every day became the best day. I didn't recognize myself anymore and not because I became a redhead and lost those thirty pounds. I had found the person who was always there. I had come full circle. I rescued myself. I found peace.

So forty, bring it! I am not afraid of you, I love you and I embrace you. I embrace you like I embrace the lines on my face, the gray in my hair, and the scars on my heart. There's no going back to where I've been. My forties will be the best decade yet!

And to you, my thirties, thank you. You showed me what true love really was. You shook me up and redefined "rolling with the punches." I learned to listen to myself and to those who were there to offer their experiences and life lessons. I learned to stop beating myself up for my mistakes, and instead celebrate each of my accomplishments. I learned to let go and trust that my life was going to be everything that I wanted to it to be.

ANA KARINA CESPEDES is Peruvian-born, Miami-raised, world-based. Accepts the never-ending task of becoming a better version of herself. Looks forward to the lesson she is here to learn, and to sharing that knowledge with the next generation of women.

57

Yesterday Thirty, Today Forty

ISIS SANTANA
Thirty-nine, Dominican

Again it is October 3rd, a special day for me for different and very important reasons: Today I celebrate Odontologist's Day, my profession, to which I have formally dedicated seventeen years of my life. There were many ups and downs and sacrifices, but I pursued my work with a lot of passion and joy.

On October 3rd, I became a mother for the first time. I had my perfect, organized life plan for the next seven or eight years when God showed me his infinite love and gave me one of his best angels as a son. Today my first son turns sixteen. I still remember his early years with a fondness and sensitivity that I don't know how to describe.

Today, October 3rd, is my last day in the hectic and edifying decade of my thirties, a decade that began with enormous expectations and even greater aspirations.

Several things came together to make this stage that ends today so special: The responsibility of raising our two children in a dignified way, the natural energy that emanates when women are productive and independent entities (which means they have to take time away from their children, sacrifice sleep, and sometimes even their health), an energy that allows you to be courageous as you make your decisions—you either move forward, or you get stuck. You always have to calculate: "What is it that I might lose? If this doesn't work out, what will I do?" In the end, I calculated my risks and realized that the only thing I could lose was a little money. Or I might complete another goal later because I needed more time. And those two variables always have a solution. So, I just took the leap. To be honest, sometimes I miss that engine that pushed me to do so much.

It has been ten years of learning and self-knowledge. I thought that when I got to my forties, I would basically be the same person. I found it very funny that many women at this age said they had become someone else, that they no longer cared so much what other people thought, that they had learned to say no, that they accepted their bodies, that they now "do what they like," are "more clear and direct," etc. It seemed like middle-aged crisis speak to me... and here I am repeating it proudly.

These years made me understand that expectations are really harmful, that they only bring disappointment and distance. In a marriage, when you expect the other person to behave or react in a particular way (according to what you think "should be"), and it doesn't happen, you are only creating distance between you and your partner. I understand that we are different and I make a great effort to just let it be. I understand that I do not want to carry the weight of high expectations. I want to feel the freedom to be who I really am, not who you think I am or want me to be. I am me... no more, no less.

I learned that we are constantly growing and transforming, not only because time passes, but also because we grow with our children as they themselves change.

I learned that changes are constant and often occur unexpectedly, and that we have to be willing to adapt to what life presents to us. Today I would like to dedicate my time to art, specifically photography, and not so much to dentistry. I spent years trying to identify my passion, considering all the options in front of me along with everyone else's opinions. I have experimented with several of my passions. This is the moment for photography, the art form that has best filled the space inside me that was seeking expression. When I look back at the last year and a half, I feel in my heart that the universe has conspired to bring me this new pursuit, so I pursue it with all my energy and really enjoy it.

Undoubtedly, some of my greatest successes come from motherhood, although over time I have come to identify the mistakes I made while raising my children—but these were minor compared to the people, students, and friends they have become.

All of these changes have marked me. I no longer feel the pressure to do or say what somebody else expects. I do not feel comfortable when someone overestimates me because that means I have to live up to their ideas and expectations. I prefer that whoever is going to love me wants me as I am. I feel much more comfortable being more direct, although I still believe that being direct doesn't mean being disrespectful, raising your voice, or controlling another person.

At the beginning of this new decade, I wish that I can simply fall in love with the new me. That I continue educating my senses and appreciate the small details and gifts of life. That I can take good care of my two-year-old baby while also balancing the demands of his siblings, and enjoy the different stages of each child's life. I want to truly dive into photography, my passion, and explore it with enthusiasm for many years to come.

I thank my thirties for transforming me from an agitated, over accommodating, demanding person to a calmer, more conscientious person, free of prejudices and limitations, more prudent, more grateful, who seeks to make peace with herself and the world as it is.

I am happy for what I have lived and learned, for how I have laughed and cried, for my achievements and failures, my children, my husband, my marriage that has overcome countless challenges, all the changes that have occurred and all the changes that will come.

Tomorrow, October 4th, I will open my heart to be reborn again and live in all the joy that the train of life brings!

ISIS SANTANA is a mother for love, dentist by profession, lover of photography, change, and life on the move.

Reading Group Guide

1. Can you relate to any of the experiences shared in this book?

2. What story struck you the most from *In Our Thirties*?

3. How do you differ from other people around the world who are living their thirties?

4. What do you think about the male perspective of life in our thirties?

5. Which expert guest piece resonated most with you and why?

6. What is the most important lesson you have learned in your thirties?

7. What are you devoting your thirties to?

8. Have you made any changes in your life since you turned thirty? Since you started reading this book? If yes, what changes have you made?

9. Pick one of these categories: People, Health, Spirit, Work, Money, Living. What could you start doing today to improve in that area of your life?

10. The following page was left blank for you to write your own story.
Would you like to share your answers to this guide and your experiences about being thirty+? Please email us at info@laurasgroi.com. We would love to hear your story!

Made in United States
North Haven, CT
12 December 2022

28634765R00113